At the
Still Point

A MEMOIR

Carol Buckley

SIMON & SCHUSTER
New York • London • Toronto
Sydney • Tokyo • Singapore

SIMON & SCHUSTER
Rockefeller Center
1230 Avenue of the Americas
New York, NY 10020

Designed by Edith Fowler
Manufactured in the United States of America

10   9   8   7   6   5   4   3   2   1

Library of Congress Cataloging-in-Publication Data

Buckley, Carol.
    At the still point : a memoir / Carol Buckley.
        p.   cm.
    1. Buckley, Carol, 1938–   . 2. Buckley, Carol,
1938–   —Mental health. 3. Buckley family.
4. Celebrities—United States—Biography. 5. Women—
United States—Biography. 6. Social workers—United
States—Biography. I. Title.
CT275.B78466A3   1996
361.3'2'092–dc20
[B]   95-35910   CIP
ISBN 0-684-80217-1

All photos courtesy of the author unless otherwise noted.
109, 110   Photo by Jay Te Winburn
162   Alfred Eisenstaedt, Life magazine, © Time Inc.
206   Photo by Jan Lukas
255   Photo by Hella Hammid

Excerpt from "Burnt Norton" in Four Quartets, copyright 1943
by T. S. Eliot and renewed 1971 by Esme Valerie Eliot, reprinted
by permission of Harcourt Brace & Company

And do not call it fixity,
Where past and future are gathered. Neither movement
    from nor towards,
Neither ascent nor decline. Except for the point, the
    still point,
There would be no dance, and there is only the dance.

T. S. Eliot

 # One

I imagine her as she must have been when they met, tiny, animated, her face turned up to his, a dimpled smile. Her eyes would have been looking down demurely. She wore a puffy white blouson, cinched waist, and skirts dancing and teasing at the ankle. And a broad-brimmed hat to keep away the sun. The Mexican sun is strong in summertime and she was there, in Mexico City, visiting her uncle, a sojourn planned away from the swampy heat of New Orleans and the malaria and yellow fever epidemics that ravaged the city. She considered herself a spinster at twenty-two. Her younger sister, Vivian, had already married.

I do not think she was there to find a husband, though she did. Not the cultivated Creole she may have imagined, not the Swiss German of her own background, but an Irishman from Texas, a brash remove from the refined, in-bred society of her native clime. And he—a thirty-six-year-old bachelor, the first son of a strong mother, the mainstay of his younger brothers and sisters, a self-made, reserved man—fell headlong in love. I don't know if there was another woman in his life before their meeting. If there was, he never said. I can't imagine it. I think of him always with her.

That he was fourteen years her senior mattered little. It was the Irish way, celibate firstborn males supporting their mothers and younger siblings well into middle age, a tradition rooted in pragmatism, initiated by an impoverished people for economic reasons and as a way of population control. And so he had been the mainstay of his family, first as a lawyer and then exploring for oil in Mexico. The law bored him; the race for oil never would, nor would the wide open frontiers of the Mexico he knew and loved. There he had survived holdups, kidnappings, and revolutions, enjoyed a mythic youth, begun his business, made his fortune. But that summer in Mexico City, it was time to marry and to love.

He was a strong man, with square shoulders, a prominent nose, and light blue eyes that masked a quick intelligence, ambition, and humor. If at first glance he looked austere, you had only to note his full, wide, sensual mouth to discover the passion there. As I remember, it was only in her presence that he smiled completely, gave himself over, let go. She bemused him, charmed him, and even in the later years when I knew them, still brought a flush to his cheeks. It wasn't that there was anything particularly remarkable about her looks—a pretty round face, auburn hair, and eyes that never decided what color to be. But she was enchanting, my mother, bubbly, flirtatious, sweet. All the things women were meant to be in that long-ago time, she was. On December 29, 1917, they married: Aloise Josephine Antonia Steiner and William Frank Buckley.

I see them still at our home, Great Elm, in Sharon, Connecticut, walking together. Sharon is in the northwestern corner of the state, in the foothills of the Berkshire

Mountains. It is dairy country, with rolling green pastures and tall stands of trees and stone fences. The pretty villages are like those pictured on Christmas cards—colonial and quaint. It was there that my father chose to bring up his growing family, a home that my brother Bill remembers as providing "unmitigated pleasure" but that I remember as quite different. My memories of the stately house and manicured grounds of Great Elm evoke a sense of solitude and of quiet, for I was born an only child in a family of ten.

"It is clear," my brother Jim writes, "that we grew up in entirely different families. I wish you could have been a member of mine. It was fun." It must have been, I understand that it was, and yet I wouldn't have traded my own childhood for anyone else's, not for Jim's or Bill's, not for any other of my remaining seven sisters' and brothers'. It was my very different childhood that freed me to reach beyond the safety of the family confines, to enter other worlds and to make lasting and deep friendships there. For in not being blessed, I was also blessed.

At Great Elm my parents walked almost daily. My mother, petite even in her stiletto heels, with earrings, pearls, rings, and the V-neck that Coco Chanel had admonished her to wear during the years they had lived in Paris. Chanel believed that small women looked taller in V-necks and so my mother's dressmaker altered the necklines of all her dresses and the base of the V was always modestly covered by a piece of lace. She had beautiful full breasts before the nursing of her many babies, a tiny waist, and slender, shapely legs. Even in old age, her legs were remarkable. And she knew it.

When they walk together, her head reaches almost to his shoulder, her face upturned. The hair is curly now, gray

9

My mother, Aloise Josephine Antonia Steiner, on her wedding day, December 29, 1917.

and slowly taking on the silver-blue tints that will domi-
nate in her later years. He wears a suit and tie and starched
shirt. He wears a hat—he, too, has an aversion to the sun.

They walk slowly up and down the drive, up to the
pool and the tennis court, to the stables, to the flower
garden beyond. They comment on this and that plant, the
forsythia—how it has filled out!—the lilacs, the yews, the
towering elms that will soon succumb to the Dutch elm
disease.

I hear her trilling laugh and sense the warm, pleased look on his face. Sometimes he pats her hand, awkwardly, diffidently. Touch does not come easily to him. Once they both bought walking sticks—quickly abandoned; once they took up dark glasses with deep green tints to make the shrubbery and lawns look even greener. At Great Elm in Sharon, Connecticut, everything is deep green because of the cascading snows and rains of winter and spring; in our winter home in South Carolina, hues softened. There was pine and sand and the perfume of magnolias, and masses of bright pastels in the camellia and azalea gardens my father designed. But I remember them walking together mostly at Great Elm.

When I left Great Elm on the first of October 1993, six weeks before my fifty-fifth birthday, I drove down the driveway behind a North American moving van, weeping like a child. I had no time, no heart, that day to remember my parents and to imagine them strolling the grounds. They were dim figures at best, my mother and father, and I knew them almost always from a distance. And so it took me by surprise—my desolation. I hadn't planned on crying. I had, after all, "left" my family behind years before—my parents, my nine older brothers and sisters, and the many caretakers of my youth. I had accepted my role in the family and worked through a range of emotions from anger to longing.

My father used to tease and say that he'd found me in a basket on the back steps, but of course I knew that wasn't so. I'd heard about my birth, and if I felt a changeling, it was not for the reasons my father gave. My parents were older by the time I came along, well into middle age, my father close to sixty. Coming at the tail end of the family,

I would lack the close bonds of the older children. My brothers and sisters would be more influenced by our parents, more enmeshed and dependent on each other for nurturing, while I was impelled to look to the world outside. Without anchor, without a true sense of belonging, I would spend my early years searching, finding, losing, and searching again. I was a 1950s girl who would ultimately become, with some resistance, a 1960s woman.

Now I choose to spend my middle years alone, to be still, to be quiet, a course that grows increasingly simple, at times gratifying, at times still wanting, for passions are not so easily packed away. My story is peculiarly American. Where else do people have such opportunity to reinvent themselves? Where else, the need? Though in my case, it was other people who invented me, gave me roles to play, made me up. Who you wanted me to be, I was; what you wanted me to do, I did. All of this, for love.

I am my parents' daughter. My mother lives in the conformation of my hands, in my facile smile and manner; my father, in the light blue eyes I use to observe the world. Like them, I made it through. I am, as well, the product of my time and of the events that shaped my life. This is the story of how I came finally to be that person.

 *Two*

Children, tomorrow at Mass I ask you all to pray for me—for my very, very special intention. Our Lord always listens, you know, and if you pray with all your hearts for the very right thing, He will answer." Her hands are beginning to show the signs of age—blue veins, knuckles lined, the translucent skin becoming slack. Her hands are never still. She plays with the pearls at her neck, she toys with her food, looking down the table at the four older ones, her "big ones": Aloise, John, Priscilla, and Jim. They will tell the middle children—Jane, Billy, and Patricia—and maybe even the babies, Reid and Maureen. News travels fast in big families.

"Yes, Mother," they chorus, though John lifts an eyebrow, hoping to make Priscilla and Jimmy laugh.

"John!" says Allie. Aloise is the oldest, and named after Mother. Being the oldest and being a girl, she is attuned to her parents in a special way. She looks at Mother in her piercing way; she sees something troubled, more than the usual worry lines.

"Are we going broke? Has Father lost his money?"

13

Father had lost his money a few times already. Once during his dramatic expulsion from Mexico and once during the Great Depression. My parents were living then in a lavish château in Chantilly, outside of Paris. As my mother remembers it, one morning Father asked her how much money she had in her checking account. My mother answered, "Four hundred dollars, Will."

"Well," he said, "Aloise, that is what we are worth!" So my mother has had worries and is probably not quite as sanguine as Father about his ability to recoup. But he does, my father always does. And things are fine again and there are trips abroad and presents and birthday parties and ponies to ride.

Mother looks now at her eldest daughter with pretend sternness: "Aloise! Of course not, we haven't lost our money. Your father is a brilliant businessman, a fact you must never forget!" Then remembering what they are talking about, for she is often distracted, she adds, "It's my intention—something I'm asking God for."

And suddenly, from nowhere, there are tears in her eyes. The children hush and look down, look away.

She fumbles for the tiny lace hanky tucked into her sleeve—it smells of her special perfume—and raises it quickly to her eyes. Brown-gray eyes that sometimes turn an olive green. "Hazel," she calls them, "not beautiful blue like your father's, or yours."

Her four blue-eyed children watch her. She is smiling now, pretend smiling. "Tomorrow is Easter!"

The meal is over, not much reason to dawdle over the floating island and vanilla wafers.

"Excuse me."

"Excuse me."

"May I be excused?"

14

"Me too?"

Grown-ups say "Excuse me"; children ask, "May I be excused?" These four are half-adult, half-child, all in their teens, too old to run from the table, so instead they hurry down the wide hall to the door leading up across the lawns to the pool and tennis court where they can talk unheeded.

"Do you think she is sick?" asks Jimmy tremulously.

"Or that Father is?" asks Priscilla.

"Pooh," says John, "of course not, dopes! It's probably just something she wants, like—I don't know—a new coat or something."

"Honestly, John," drawls Aloise, "Mother would never have us pray for a new coat!"

"A ring," says Priscilla, "a beautiful new ring."

"Dummy—of course not. Father gives her lots of rings. It's something much more important," says Allie. And sensing that John is becoming restless—he's a redhead and often gets that way around his brothers and sisters—she turns to him and asks, "What would Mother want more than anything else, John? Think about it."

"A . . ."

"A baby!" exclaims Priscilla.

"A baby, of course!" says Allie, and gives Priscilla an approving look.

Priscilla is pleased as pie. When Aloise approves, which is seldom, you are apt to feel very special.

"Of course, a baby—Maureen is almost six years old!"

"I think Mother has enough babies," says John, wrinkling his nose. "Nine is enough!"

"Mother wants another baby," says Jimmy, secure in his conviction that he is right because he knows he is his mother's favorite—her favorite out of the whole bunch. She often says so.

15

"We'll tell the others," says Allie, "Jane and Billy and Patricia."

"And Reid and Maureen." Priscilla pauses and puts on a grown-up look, "Maybe Maureen is too young to know about babies . . ."

"Honestly, Pitts! Maureen is six whole years old!"

Allie calls Priscilla "Pitts." Soon everyone will.

On Easter Sunday morning in the spring of 1938, eleven Buckleys file into the two front pews of Saint Bernard's Catholic Church. Father is beginning to grow bald, a pink tonsure growing at the back of his head. He kneels and stands upright, never bending. Mother, black lace mantilla pinned to her graying, marcelled waves, bows over her rosary, her lips moving in supplication. The nine children— five brown heads, three red, one blond—pray also. So does their governess, Mademoiselle Bouchex; so do the two Mexican nurses, Nana and Felipa. The children have told

Mother and Father, eight little Buckleys, and Nana at the Hotel Grunwald, Grindelwald, Switzerland, in the late 1920s.

them of Mother's intention. God is being besieged in many languages.

I imagine them praying together in the church in Sharon, but perhaps they were abroad. Maybe it was in London they went to Easter Mass and prayed together. I know that in 1938 my sister Aloise, a student at Smith College, was on her way to France for the summer. I don't think she had been suspended yet for ringing the school alarms or for changing the exam dates on the classroom blackboards. Aloise was fiercely independent and actually remained that entire year in France. I know that my parents were concerned about getting her back to the United States and to Smith before the outbreak of war in Europe.

John was attending Yale, Jim a senior at Millbrook, and Priscilla was at Nightingale-Bamford in New York. Jane and Patricia and Billy, resentfully, attended English boarding schools. My father was an education junkie—he didn't think it possible to have enough, and he believed as well that no one was properly educated without spending at least two or three years abroad studying the classics. Reid and Maureen, the young ones, were still at home, being tutored and cared for by Nana and Felipa and by Mademoiselle Bouchex.

What I do know for certain is that the children must have prayed very hard for my mother's intention, obviously cumulatively harder than my poor mother, who was imploring her God to spare her another pregnancy. My brothers and sisters won. And that is how I came to be.

The other story I knew from early on—this was a story about being a very good Catholic (most of our family stories had morals to them)—was that my mother's obstetrician, being a good Catholic himself and fearing that

Mother would die if she brought me to term, referred her to another physician. He lectured my mother about the dangers of childbirth at her advanced age, and also warned that given the fact that she had had a reparatory operation after Maureen's birth, her womb and cervix and vagina being sewed up with permanent stitches, I would have to break through these in birth. When she mounted the examining table, the consulting doctor began fiddling with some unusual instruments, and my mother, suspecting that he was about to attempt an abortion, leaped off the table and fled.

When I first heard this story, I was very proud. I was very, very proud as a little girl and later as a teenager that my mother had not aborted me, because abortion was a sin. When I repeated it years later to a psychiatrist, I was very angry, in the grips of a numbing depression that left me empty and self-loathing. I was close to hating my mother as well for her seeming rejection of me, and close to death myself. Now, as a middle-aged woman, well past the age of forty-three, I think of her, tired and exhausted from pregnancies and babies, wanting time with my father, wanting time for herself, fearing for her life and praying to the God she believed in with a full heart: Oh, God, sweet Jesus, don't let this be, don't let me be pregnant—don't let me die!

And she almost did. At least that is what I was told. The doctor said, "Mrs. Buckley, you have a little girl with dimples." That in itself must have been a disappointment, for I was meant to be a boy to round out the family: five daughters, five sons. A short time later, just before she lapsed into a coma, my mother heard the nurse say to the doctor, "What a shame to die and leave ten children!" And the doctor was very angry with the nurse, and that was all my mother remembered. So that's about it for my origins, that I nearly killed my mother.

Three

My brothers and sisters tell me that soon after my birth, in the winter of 1939, I crossed the ocean on the virgin voyage of the *Paris*. My brother Reid remembers that "a great hurricane shook the sea. Oh! Oh! Oh! Oh!— wept the *Paris*, in all her creaky wooden fittings. Dining room chairs bolted to the floors were ripped out by their iron roots. People walked a drunken trail across the decks, and then, as the ship heaved in a heavy list to the other side, danced teetering like sandpipers across to the opposite bulkhead. Mother prayed. Nana crossed herself a thousand times and moaned. Maureen and I (Carol was an infant strapped into her crib) watched with fearless joy out the dark portholes as the sea rose tumultously and hung black and tremendous above the reach of our eyes, and then crashed down on the sides of the ship and blurred our vision in swirling foam—great mountains of moving water gaping open in deep troughs down which the *Paris* plummeted."

If Reid's account is true—Reid is a novelist and has a good imagination—I'm glad I was too young to remember

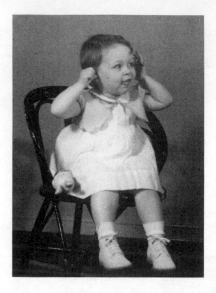

*Poppy's enchanted listener
(the author, aged two years).*

the voyage. My crib was secured to the stateroom wall. Jane and Billy and Patricia had great fun loosening it and letting it roll back and forth to the swell of the mighty waves. They *said* I liked it, they said I smiled and chuckled, but then, we are a family full of tales and stories, some of them most certainly apocryphal. My mother, for instance, persisted in her belief that she was directly descended from William Tell. Nothing would dissuade her of this belief, not even the fact that William Tell is a fictional character.

My father's stories, though, were the best. I think the storytelling came from the Irish in him although we never speak much in my family about our Irishness; we are only half Irish after all, but, oh, my, how it dominates! It shines in our very blue eyes, in our restraint, in our humor and articulateness, and in the tears that often shimmer but are seldom allowed down. Though Father was often withdrawn and shy, he loved stories and he told them well. And even as he repeated them over and over again, I was never bored. His favorite stories were about his early days in Texas and in Mexico, and about rattlesnakes and bandits and kidnappers and *his* father, a real Texas sheriff, who knew Pat Garrett (who killed Billy the Kid!) and who never carried a gun. My father had been kidnapped and held for ransom by a villainous group of Mexican bandits for one whole week until his friend Mr. Velasco rescued him. And once, he acted as translator for emissaries of the American government at a meeting with the famous outlaw and revolutionary, Zapata! My father was bigger than life, braver than Gary Cooper and John Wayne and Randolph Scott, and more handsome, too.

"Well, now . . ." my poppy says, dragging out the "well" until it almost makes two syllables. It is one of his favorite

21

storytelling phrases. We are sitting at the head of the long, gleaming dining room table at Great Elm; evening shadows dim the summer light outside so that the candles down the table glimmer and dance. I have been allowed downstairs in my pajamas to kiss good night. When my father says, "Well, now . . ." I feel excitement, and his eyes take on a look of fun. This is the best part of the story, the part that comes after, "Well, now . . ." After "well now," the happy ending happens: my poppy kills the rattlesnake, fools the bandits, escapes his kidnappers. God is in His heaven and I will always be safe with Poppy.

I am in his lap. I smell soap and a slightly sweaty male smell. He lets me play with his chin and scrape the bristles there. When I am little he lets me play at anything and never criticizes. I am not one bit afraid of him, though sometimes other people seem to be. Some people act strained in his presence and try to impress him. But with my poppy, I just am.

Well, now . . .

It wasn't only our wild Texas origins that made us Buckleys different; we were *proud* to be different. "The Buckleys against the world," we used to say. In Sharon, Connecticut, at Great Elm, we lived among staid, moneyed Episcopalians—old Yankee families, liberal Republicans given to one or two offspring at most. We were ten and Roman Catholic and boisterously conservative. I don't think it was merely that wherever we lived, we subscribed to different political beliefs or belonged to a "foreign" religion, or even that there were so very many of us. I think it was a Buckley tradition—always to be on the other (or different) side. It runs in our blood and manifests itself in a strong debating gene. We Buckleys can argue anyone into a corner—even when we are absolutely misguided and wrong.

My County Cork great-grandfather, a Protestant, married a Catholic girl and the story goes that he emigrated to Canada only after bopping a fellow Orangeman on the head with a plowshare for insulting her. He didn't waste much time waiting to see whether the fellow recovered or not but packed up his belongings and sailed away to the New World. In Canada he owned a farm and lived a productive life, despite the fact that he remained unenlightened and Protestant all his remaining years. When I heard this story, my mother always hastened to add that Great-grandfather Buckley did finally see the light and became a Roman Catholic on his deathbed. Father whispered in my ear, "He must have been unconscious when he converted." My poppy gives me a great wink when he says this and my mother cries, "Will!" but I see that she is smiling.

His son, my grandfather John, would leave the safety of his farm in Canada for the wilds of Texas. When he told his mother-in-law that he was thinking of doing so, she pointed to a graveyard on the hill and said, "I would rather see my daughter there than in that wild and heathen place." He didn't pay much mind, and within the year, my grandparents arrived in a wagon with all their belongings in the border town of Washington-on-Brazos. There Grandfather Buckley set about raising sheep in cattle country, not a popular thing to do, running for office with the support of the Mexican majority but not of his fellow white settlers, and carrying out his duties as sheriff while refusing absolutely to wear a gun.

His oldest son, my father, was pretty independent himself and carried on the tradition of holding unpopular positions. His dear friend Cecilio Velasco described my father's confrontations with the profit-hungry American oil community in Mexico City: "At every meeting that took place in the Petroleum Club, W.F.B. found himself conducting a heated battle in an attempt to make his fellow Americans understand that they were in Mexico, a free and sovereign nation that demanded and deserved respect." My father's defense of Mexico and of Mexican values so angered the oilmen that he was finally expelled from the club as a "pernicious and quarrelsome individual."

He would continue to goad the oil establishment. He was a risk-taker and preferred to win the gamble, make the deal, outsmart. Learning early the whimsy of black gold, he traveled the world buying mineral rights, thousands upon thousands of acres of mineral rights. These he then sold at a premium to the giant oil companies, retaining royalties on every barrel produced. It was a simple concept, but at that time it was uniquely his. The oil companies took the financial risks of drilling dry holes. If, on the other hand, they struck oil, they had to share their profits with my father. No wonder they resented him.

It was that aspect of the business that my father enjoyed, playing David to their Goliath. He preferred the contest to the actual moneymaking part of it. He liked to have money to spend, mostly on his children and homes. But in other ways he was not acquisitive. Every ten years or so my mother forced him to purchase new clothes. He did, often ordering four suits of exactly the same fit and stripe. Father had little respect for money as such and was open-handed, generous to a fault. Not for him the penurious Puritan attitudes of the wealthy Yankee families of Sharon.

And then there was our mother, the unapologetic New Orleans belle. My mother's family stories paled by com-

parison to Father's. That she and her sister had been chosen to present a bouquet of flowers to Robert E. Lee's
nephew, Fitzhugh, impressed me not at all. Nor did her
pretensions to class or her obscure family connection to the
Lees (and to William Tell). What did impress me, though,
and what filled me with longing was her sweet aura. My
mother wore silks and makeup and pearls and smelled of
French perfume. When she left the room, her scent lin-
gered; when she spoke and laughed, she made melodies of
sound. The other women who lived up and down the green
pinned their hair in buns and put their feet in sensible
shoes. They were plainspoken, plain-faced, austerely
dressed, and yet, for all their Yankee restraint, I found
them condescending.

Sharon was a very small town in those days and maintained rigid class distinctions. When my parents first moved
there in 1922, the few ladies who called at the house simply
left their cards. In those days, calling cards had a language
of their own and a couple of them left cards with a corner
folded, which expressed the wish that Mother need not call
back. Snubbing was still a part of this stratified system. My
poor young mother, friendly, gregarious, was excluded for
being Catholic, for being southern, and for being married
to a brash Texan with no proper Wall Street connections.

But by the time of my birth, my mother had made a
number of women friends in Sharon. How could a woman
as pleasing as she fail to? Many of these women were older,
more my father's generation. I recall those daunting ladies.
I was always made to curtsy to them when I said hello, and
to ask "how do you do?" and never ever say "hi." They
were quite formal, reserved, and they spoke quietly; they
didn't "chatter." My mother, on the other hand, never
stopped.

"Aloise, must you speak so much?" my father would say. And with a little moue, Mother would stop talking for a minute or two, at least until another irrepressible thought popped into her head. She was quite vain. She wore clicking high heels and renewed her lipstick at least once an hour. My father said that putting on lipstick in public was akin to brushing your teeth in public. My mother would giggle at this, look a little hurt, and continue to paint her lips a deep rose.

In Camden, South Carolina, where my parents began spending their winters soon after my birth, our friends were also different. They were Presbyterian and Episcopalian, and were conservative Democrats, and sportsmen, somewhat suspicious of the "overly educated," not to mention the foreign-language-speaking. At this time there were at least three language groups in my family: French-speaking Aloise, John, Priscilla, and Jim, who had spent their early years in France and were cared for by Mademoiselle Bouchex; Spanish-speaking Jane, Billy, Patricia, and Reid, who had Mexican nurses; English-speaking Maureen, who was stubborn and wanted to be "an American"; and nonspeaking infant, me.

Camden is in a flat section of the state, filled with virgin pine and oak and towering magnolia and holly. Everywhere there is sand and, underneath the sand, porous red clay. It is sunny and dry in winter, a mecca for hunting and racing horses, for bird-shooting and golf. And though my parents were not athletic themselves, they were born southerners and delighted to return to the gracious and gentle tempo of southern life and manners. It was in Camden that my mother made her closest friends and seemed most at home. Mother had hated the long Connecticut winters and had felt isolated there with my father away on his month-long business trips to Venezuela, England, and France. In Camden, Mother was finally relieved of many of her maternal duties. Eight of the children were now away at boarding school and college. She was happy, too, at last to have my father to herself.

He was semiretired now, carrying on his business by telephone with the office in New York. Sometimes his colleagues visited Camden for marathon strategy sessions. My father was never happier than when he was surrounded by his old business friends, men whose history went back to his early days in Mexico and Venezuela. These were the men he knew and understood and laughed with. The Camden and Sharon friends were really my mother's, and he remained somewhat shy and reserved in their presence.

For all that my parents were happy in Camden, I still felt our differentness. My playmates' parents were just slightly older than my own older brothers and sisters; they were horsemen, sportsmen, heavy drinkers, and when not in the field, they partied or played poker well into the night. These were mostly Yankees, wealthy men who had never done a day's work and spent their lives marrying, divorcing, foxhunting, and training their retrievers. That was the "fast" Camden crowd; my parents preferred the honest-to-God southerners. They were a gracious, gregarious bunch, many related to one another: cousins—kissing and actual. They took you in, but they also let you know that you didn't quite belong, and occasionally they reminded you where you had come from. I remember one old gentleman saying to me of his thousand-acre-plus plantation: "Well, honey, we're just plain country folk. We just have a big ole farm, not an ee-state like your daddy."

Most Camden homes had two or three pointers, short-haired freckled dogs, and retrievers, either Chesapeakes or

Labs, and wide center halls filled with hunting gear and the smell of pine kindling—they call it "fatwood"—snapping and popping in the fireplaces. Camden families definitely did not have Mexican nurses and French governesses; they had "help," not servants, and their big houses were just slightly falling apart, many in need of a coat of paint. Our house shone and was fresh-painted. Some of our servants moved seasonally, up north to Sharon in late May, down south to Camden in early December, to open up and prepare the houses for us.

Patricia, Jane, Reid, and Maureen keep me entertained on the "patio" at Great Elm.

 *Four*

My father often said things that hurt my
mother. I remember her crying at times. The very things
that charmed him about her—her gaiety, her extroversion
and charm—also irritated him. He was a man who needed
times of silence, the space to reflect and to think. When my
father was angered, his mouth went straight as a ruler. And
yet he never stayed angry at Mother for long. He was
enchanted by her and touched by the uncertain, vulnerable
part of her that cried out for reassurance and love and
ensured his place as her protector. Once, Mother apologized to him for being pregnant so often, and my father
answered, "Whenever I see a pregnant woman, I want to
tip my hat to her." That was lucky. My mother bore him
eleven children.

There was a little redheaded sister, Mary Anne, who
was born between Patricia and Reid. My mother was nursing her when she felt the little girl turn cold and blue. "Blue
babies," they called them, and in those days they had no
cure for them. My sister Priscilla remembers Father returning to Great Elm from New York City and mounting the

29

stairs to go to his room. She ran up to him and excitedly asked, "Did Mother have the new baby? Do we have a new baby?"

My father turned his head to the wall and wept. Priscilla still looks a little sad, or ashamed, when she tells this story. In my family, if anything you have done has caused any other member of the family pain, you feel very bad, and guilty, as if you had sinned. Within the family, discussion is permitted and opinions may be stated, but dissension is immediately quashed, as if the structure of the family might fall apart should overt disagreement be voiced. It is safer, therefore, not to speak, particularly if the truth might hurt.

Topics of a personal nature were vigilantly suppressed, and so my early years were often spent wondering and worrying but never quite daring to question. My big brothers and sisters came and went—sometimes the house was bursting with them; sometimes it was empty, with only Maureen and me. By the time I was five years old, I had only this sister left at home, and she would soon leave for the Ethel Walker School. My parents traveled and entertained or dined out two or three times a week. Among the things I never seemed to know or understand was where everyone went. Often I wept disconsolately when a brother or sister left without saying good-bye. Sometimes my nurse disappeared too, on vacation. For a little girl, too many disappearances, too many mysteries and losses.

My dog, Prince, a velvety Irish setter, is at the vet's. At least I think he's at the vet. He has been there a long time, but I am too young to measure days and weeks. I am afraid to ask about him, and no one says. I know only that one morning when I went to feed him before school, Prince had

30

trouble standing. He stumbled and weaved getting from his bed to the kennel gate to greet me. Prince's bed is made of a wooden barrel on stilts to keep the damp out, and it is filled with linseed, an oily cotton matting that my father says is good for dogs' coats. My Irish setter has a wonderful coat, coppery and bright. Prince tries to wag his tail; he falls. There is bubbly white foam at his mouth. "Oh, Prince," I say. "Stay there, boy. I'll get help—I'll get the doctor."

My dog is so sick! I understand that, for I have read about distemper in one of my dog books. I run back up to the kitchen and ask Ella, our maid, and Sally, the cook, please to get Leslie, please to ask him to take Prince to the vet. Please, Prince is sick! I swallow back tears, I feel nauseated. Ella and Sally look perturbed, and Ella puts her arm around my shoulders. I pull back—sympathy will make me cry even harder. She tells me that Jeff is ready to take me to school. Jeff is our butler and always drives me to school on his way to the market.

"It's all right, little miss, I just know he'll be all right," says Ella. "Yes, honey, your dog he gonna be just fine," says Sally.

I cannot bear that I must go with Jeff and leave my dog behind, but I do. I am a good girl and do what I am told; it never occurs to me to ask to stay with Prince. It never occurs to me to tell my parents.

Our gardener, Leslie, drove Prince to the vet. Prince never came back. He was never spoken of again. Some months later, after praying for him every night and every Sunday at Mass, and longing for news of him, I told Priscilla she could tell Mother and Father that I knew Prince had died and was never coming back. I didn't want to hurt them by having them have to hurt me by telling me the truth.

It was a complicated system, communicating in my family. That is why we prefer to write when the matter is personal. If you want to express love, you write it. If you want to express concern, you write it. It is just as embarrassing to say something nice directly to someone as to say something critical because it is the expression of any emotion whatsoever that causes discomfort. "Don't make personal remarks," I was admonished by both my parents. This rule ranked somewhere close to "Children should be seen and not heard" (Father and Mother) and "Little pitchers have big ears" (brothers and sisters).

 *Five*

We spent the winter of 1943 in Mexico City. My memories of Mexico are mostly of my beloved nurse, Pupa, my mommy, my poppy, and my sister Maureen. Father looked very, very happy to be back after so many years away. He had started his business there as a young man and planned to live in Mexico City. Unfortunately he took an unpopular political stand, refusing to support the Obregon government and was banished by the state of Mexico as persona non grata.

We moved into a big dark house—my parents, my sister Priscilla, just graduated from Smith College, and Maureen. Jane, Bill, Patricia, and Reid visited at different times. I was four years old, just becoming self-aware, just beginning to want to be one with my big boisterous brothers and sisters—"*los grandes,*" my nurse called them.

I knew them all by name, all except for my sister Aloise who had married a man called Ben—Aloise, Maureen told me, had gone away in a car with Ben Heath to the air force—and my two oldest brothers, John and Jim. I couldn't remember John and Jim at all and often got their pictures confused. There was something called "the war" going on. The war put my brother John in the cavalry and would send him to a place called North Africa. And my brother Jim was to be put in the navy, aboard an LST in the Pacific. In my mind, big hands had come out of the sky and picked up my two brothers and Ben and plunked them down in faraway places. I believed the hands belonged to a man that my poppy disliked called president-roosevelt, or sometimes that-rascal-franklin-roosevelt. My mother looked sad when John and Jimmy's names were mentioned.

I was becoming a pest, and often it was suggested by *los grandes* that I shut my ears, shut my mouth, or just plain go away—it was something they called "grown-up time." I hated grown-up time. How it stung me to be removed from their lively, laughing camaraderie! Sometimes they teased, telling me about the giant Mexican tarantulas that crawled about the ceilings at night; sometimes they were nice and treated me to ice cream and told me fairy tales and sang to me. If I didn't yet understand how different we were from our neighbors, I was beginning to understand how different I was from "them," the big ones. They dined with my parents; I ate with my nurse. They stayed up late; I went to bed before the sun was down. And worst of all, I had naps—the only person in the whole household to have naps!

Every morning after breakfast I was allowed to run into my parents' bedroom. Mostly I liked jumping up and down on my poppy's stomach, a rather large one. Once I made the mistake of calling it a *barriga,* which is a very rude word, and had my mouth washed out with soap as punishment. Father thought it quite amusing, but Pupa was shocked and embarrassed at my crass language—picked up, of course, from her. Mommy told Maureen and me

"Nancy" stories, tales of a very brave little girl who worked as a Confederate spy and whose adventures Mother made up every morning over her breakfast tray. Sometimes I was allowed to drink her leftover orange juice mixed with water. It tasted awful—diluted and bitter—but I never let on, for to be with my mother was a special treat. That Maureen was also allowed to be there made her special too.

Maureen was six years older than I, and quite my opposite. She was serious, honest, funny, and very modest. Where I was devious, she was direct; where I was cowardly, she was brave. She didn't seem overly fond of me in those days. She preferred Jimmy, her springer spaniel. But if she didn't seem to like me much then, she was ferocious

A soulful Maureen, sixteen years old.

in her protectiveness, and I learned during that year in
Mexico that I could always, always count on her.

*Pupa, which is what I call my nurse Felipa, takes me every
morning to a gloomy house, to "play." We walk there,
bundled up in our coats against the dry, cold Mexican
winter. The building that we go to has an iron gate. Pupa
rings the bell and I can hear it inside, very far away, sounding ding, ding, ding.*

*A woman finally comes. She is in black and does not
look at me. She nods and says, "Buenos días," to Felipa,
and takes my hand, and leads me swiftly across the cold
courtyard. I race to keep up, the tiles are slippery, the
woman unsmiling. Inside is what I dread the most: the
cold, the dark, and the children.*

*They are little girls too, with black, black hair and
black eyes. Sometimes they giggle at me; sometimes they
just turn their backs and play. I don't know which is worse,
which I hate the most. I don't know why I am here.*

*The woman in black takes off my coat. It is a heavy
navy wool, and underneath it my sweater sleeves have rid-
den up and bunched. I am wearing a tomato-red sweater
and a tiny plaid skirt with suspenders. The straps fall
down; sometimes the little girls pull them down. I don't
care, because I have brought my own friends to play with.
Quickly, before the lady takes my coat away, I cry, "Por
favor, señorita, por favor déjame . . ." and dig into the
pockets for these favorite possessions: Snow White and the
Seven Dwarfs. I know the girls are envious of them; the
figures are special—they are American!*

*They are made of lead and painted bright colors ex-
cept where I have chewed them. In those days I put everything in my mouth and bite on it—erasers, the corners of*

pillows, my sweater sleeves. I play with Snow White by myself, sitting on the floor; I play with Dopey and Grumpy. I sing "Hi-ho, hi-ho, it's off to work we go," as loud as I can—it is the only English I know how to speak. The little girls laugh.

After a very long time we say a prayer and get juice. It comes in little cans and tastes tinny. On special days there are squares of candy, sticky, milky candy so sweet that it hurts your teeth. After that, it's nap time. We put away our toys and lie down on flat mats with blankets over us. I love nap time because soon after, Pupa will come, and I can go home for lunch.

One day when we were almost home, just across the street from our front door, I put my hands into the pockets of my coat and—they were gone! My Snow White! My Dwarfs! I was disconsolate. I wept, I wailed. I cried myself to sleep without eating lunch.

"Well, now"—that was all Maureen needed to hear. The next morning, with Felipa holding one hand and Maureen the other, I was marched back to school, and Maureen who hated speaking Spanish and always pretended she didn't know how, unleashed a torrent of indignant reproaches. I do believe she used the word *"ladrones"*—thieves, brigands! And that very day, before school was over, Snow White and her Dwarfs were returned to me by a very subdued teacher. I don't know how she retrieved them, but I do know that I never had to go back to the play school again. What a victory! What a wonderful thing to have a sister Maureen!

 *Six*

We returned to Camden the next winter, and there I was reintroduced to my sister Aloise. Now I know from photographs that I was a flower girl in Allie and Ben's wedding two years earlier. I am an imp in a tiny satin dress, and in one wedding photo my tongue is sticking straight out at the camera. I also remember coloring something for her as a gift, and the gravity with which she thanked me. But all memory of her had vanished during the year in Mexico. Aloise, the eldest, was of the French-English speaking bunch of the family; she was not fluent in Spanish. We met at the breakfast table in Camden. I suppose I was five, or maybe six.

"Good morning, Carolita," says Allie, "I'm your sister Aloise."

I regard her in stony silence.

"Do you remember me?"

Silence.

"Are you enjoying your breakfast?"

Silence.

38

Flower girl at my sister Aloise's wedding, December 1942 (Kam-schatka, Camden, South Carolina).

"Would you like me to let you eat your breakfast in peace?"

Silence.

I eat my scrambled eggs. Also my delicious ham. And toast with jam. The woman orders only juice and coffee.

She picks up a newspaper and buries her head in it. She lights a cigarette and blows smoke. She acts as though I'm not even there.

I drop my spoon to get her attention. She doesn't look up. I drop my knife, on the floor this time, with a clang. I think she hears it, but she doesn't move a muscle. My shoulders just reach the table so I put my elbows on it and my chin, which is bad manners. She doesn't say anything. I take the edge of the table with my hands and rock back, then let the front chair legs fall—thud! That is bad behavior. She doesn't even notice. . . .

All right, if that's how it's going to be! I clear my throat, and smiling most graciously, as graciously as I know how, I say in a loud voice, "A mí me encanta el jamón!"—I find ham simply enchanting!

She peers over the paper, black brows lifted, deep blue eyes round with surprise. "Were you speaking to me, Carolita?"

In Camden I had school friends to play with and a close-to-normal life. Kamschatka was a wonderful, airy house with porches all around and purple wisteria perfuming the air. I always believed that this house was especially mine, for it had been purchased at the time of my birth and most of my years there were spent as an only child. I roamed the house at will, playing with my mother's curios: porcelain cups and saucers, tiny scent bottles, silver lockets containing curls of hair and the dim, painted faces of loved ones disappeared. Opening the drawers of polished highboys and chests and antique secretaries, I uncovered a treasure trove of little objects, and my mother never seemed to mind that I played with them endlessly, arranging and rearranging them.

Every evening as Mother dressed for dinner, Pupa brought me down in my pajamas to say good night. There, in Mother's pretty dressing room, the scent of her Mary Chess bath oil perfuming the air, I watched her make up and put on her jewelry. I was enchanted by the beautiful glittering stones lying in their felt-covered drawers. Sometimes my mother would turn to me and say, "Carolita, what earrings should I wear tonight?"

"The green ones?"

"Emeralds, honey? Are they the prettiest color for my blue dress? Or . . . ?"

Then I would answer, "The blue ones, the blue and the shiny ones, Mother."

And when she would nod and reach for the sapphire and diamond earrings, I felt very proud to be so adult and to have such good taste.

This was my time to be with Mother. After Maureen left for boarding school, the breakfast visits and Nancy stories had stopped abruptly. I didn't care. I had lots of people to take care of me—Pupa and Mademoiselle, Ella and Jeff and Sally and Elizabeth. And even George Tucker, our groom. Forbidden to chew gum, I often visited George in the stables and stole (and chewed) the clumps of gum he had stuck under a table.

It is Christmas, maybe 1945 or 1946, and I am allowed to stay up almost to midnight Mass. I have had an extra-long nap. I sleep in a front bedroom on the roomy third floor. I have white wallpaper with roses twining up and down. I have a rose rug, too, and white-painted furniture. Pupa is trying to braid my hair, but it is quite slippery and not thick enough. The silky bows keep falling off.

Downstairs I can hear my mother running up and

down the stairs, her heels tap-tapping, her voice calling out, "Oh, Elizabeth? . . . Ella!" My mother's calling voice has a lilt to it. The house is bustling and for two days there has been the smell of baking and of the furniture oil that Jeff rubs up and down the banisters, polishing the pine glossy-smooth. The first floor is full of pots of ugly red flowers—I am insulted to be reminded not to eat them!

In the downstairs dining room, the mahogany table— the big one, not the one I sit at—has been extended its full length. The walls are covered with a creamy magnolia-print paper, gilt mirrors, and an oil portrait of a soulful young Andrew Jackson, turning his face to the left so that his dueling scar doesn't show. On the table is a silver epergne filled with fruit and nuts nestled in little clusters on glossy magnolia leaves. There are silver bowls of after-dinner mints and bonbons. Ella has set the table three or four times. She is a perfectionist. She asks me please to go play somewhere else—she can't concentrate while I'm there. She floats red camellias in a pair of Lalique bowls.

Jeff is also too busy to play, vacuuming up a storm— loud, so people can hear that he's working; Jeff does work hard, except when he has a sleepy smile on his face and his breath smells funny. Sally, in the kitchen, who is usually nice to me, tells me plainly to "git." She won't even give me a bite of corn bread stuffing or a nibble of pumpkin pie crust. Sweat streams down her face, and the kitchen smells of that, and cinnamon.

Maureen won't play with me because Patricia is home from Vassar. Patricia is her favorite sister. Maureen is my favorite sister, though I think this Christmas maybe I'll make Jane my favorite. Jane has a long brown pageboy, wears red lipstick, and has boyfriends. She is beautiful and very rebellious. She goes to Smith College and smokes!

Behind father's back, of course. My father says smoking is cheap and bad for your health—what does he know! Reid, who sometimes plays with me, is awful. He always is when "the boys" are home. He always wants to be with them, impressing them. They aren't impressed, but they seem to like him all right. John does a lot of talking, and so does Billy. They talk talk that you can't get into, batting sentences back and forth, clipped and fast like a Ping-Pong ball. Jimmy is quiet and laughs at their jokes. Pitts hangs out with the boys.

She goes shooting with John, walking through the crisp woods, waiting for the dogs to freeze in point. Sometimes, if I promise to be very quiet, I'm allowed to go and watch. When the dogs point, rigid and trembling with excitement, I hold my breath. There will be a tremendous flutter as the covey breaks, and then the pow-pow-pow *of shotguns, and the smoky smell of spent powder. The dogs on command—"Fetch it! Fetch it!" they're ordered—race to retrieve the quarry, then return to John and Priscilla and delicately drop the birds at their feet, not a feather misplaced, not a tooth mark to be found. They wag their tails for a job well done, and I am allowed to pat them thank you. We bring home the quail and have it for Sunday brunch: roast quail, bacon, grits, and broiled tomatoes. Pitts plays golf, too.*

My other sisters just ride horses, but mostly Jane and Patricia "rest" in their bedroom upstairs, reading and smoking. Sometimes I'm allowed in, sometimes, of course, it's grown-up time, the time they don't want me to hear the things they say. They're right, because sometimes I tell Mademoiselle or Pupa, and of course I always tell Maureen. Always.

Mostly, I feel very, very excited, because of Santa

Claus. He almost comes just for me, now. I'm the only one who gets a stocking, though the stocking is always a disappointment. It has things like oranges in it, and walnuts! I wish it had gum. My sister Patricia has shining red hair and a temper to match and likes to break rules: she always gives me gum, and anything else I want! I like it that they are all home. I hate it that they are all home. I think they like me, but only for very short periods of time. Lots of the time I'm "in the way."

Our Mexican nurses, Nana and Pupa, are planning a "posada" for after dinner and before midnight Mass. I wonder how many other people in South Carolina parade around after Christmas Eve dinner, chanting lugubriously in Spanish that there is no room in the inn? We march in a dolorous line, singing off-key, and Nana, who is always self-important, plays Joseph, knocking at the inn doors and getting turned away. When Mary and Joseph finally find a room in the stable, the posada is over. We are blindfolded and given brooms to try to knock down and break the piñata. I, of course, always fail, though everyone is rooting for me, and piggy Reid finally steps in and knocks it down.

Oh, goodness, the things Reid does! Once he walked around all summer in Sharon, saying the Mass in Latin in every single Great Elm room—and there must have been thirty at least if you count the servants' quarters. He wanted to "purify" the house! My father says he danced and sang in England once, in front of a whole crowd of people waiting to see the king. That was the same king that Billy wrote to, asking that he repay Britain's war debt to the United States. Reid was the first member of the Millbrook football team to rub black grease under his eyes to shade them from the glare. Just like the pros. Unfortunately he left quite a lot of grease on his hands and kept fumbling the ball. He also rode horses recklessly and often fell off. "There goes Buckley back for blood," cried a by-stander at the Goshen Horse Show. Reid positively floated on that one for the rest of the summer.

But right now, tonight, Reid has stolen the limelight at the wrong time. I am meant to break the piñata, not attention-grabbing Reid. I am the baby—the piñata is for me! He looks puzzled and hurt when no one applauds him.

I don't care! The piñata just has more oranges and walnuts. I know it is Nana who has filled it (and probably my stocking too!). Nana is Felipa's enemy. They have lived and worked side by side for over twenty years, but they don't speak. Nana is mean, and makes up to Mother all the time in a phony way that even I can recognize. And Mother falls for it!

My mother even falls for Father's jokes! Sometimes I think she's dim-witted—and sometimes I think she pre-tends. To please him. My mother works hard at pleasing everyone and it makes her tired. My father, however, looks pleased just to see me; his eyes light up when I enter the room. He knows that I'm brave and good even though he never says so—to say is to spoil and a "spoiled brat" is the worst thing you can be in my family.

Father won't be smiling at me for very long. He will become a cripple from strokes. He will sit in a wheelchair, and sometimes for no apparent reason tears will roll down his cheeks. But tonight I don't know that, tonight after the posada, the colored carolers will come from the First Zion Baptist Church, Jeff's church.

We hear them first outside on the drive, great deep baritones and lush contraltos: "Go Tell It on the Moun-tain." Mother acts surprised and runs to the door to invite them in. Then it's "Little David, Play on Your Harp,"

"Nobody Knows the Troubles I've Seen," and then "Silent Night" and "Joy to the World!" Mother always asks for one of the spirituals a second time. If they choose to sing "Sometimes I Feel Like a Motherless Child," tears come to her eyes. Me too—songs about mothers make me very sad. The carolers are invited to the kitchen for eggnog and fruitcake. Their eggnog is on the kitchen table in a very nice glass bowl. Ours is in the dining room in a great silver bowl that sweats from the icy cream inside. There is a discreet envelope by the toaster made out to First Zion. Everyone says "Merry Christmas!" and the carolers leave by the back door. Some of them haven't smiled from be-

When I was left alone at Great Elm for the summer, the staff became my surrogate family. From left to right: Jeff Boykin, "Belle," Ella Whittaker, and Elizabeth Carlos, at my sister Jane's wedding (Great Elm, Sharon, Connecticut).

ginning to end; others make little bows, tipping their heads, and smile constantly. No one, black or white, seems embarrassed by this charade. It seems quite natural and spontaneous; it all seems a part of Christmas cheer.

When the carolers leave, I am taken to bed. The mysteries of midnight Mass and the scents of candle wax and evergreens and the sound of voices soaring in the black night are not yet for me. No stirring Father Burke sermon. They said he came from vaudeville and I believe it. What an Irishman he is! What a charmer, though I resent him because he always pinches my dimples and says he is going to fill them with plaster of Paris. When I make my first confession at age seven, he gives me absolution and a penance of three Hail Marys . . . and a can of plaster of Paris.

I cry. I don't want to go to bed. I want to be with them, los grandes. Always—I just always want to be one of them. And it never happens. Pupa takes me upstairs and I cry and kick and scream, and John, who is a sucker for distressed little children, comes up and tells me a story about the Lone Ranger. He is another of my heroes. And then—this is very typical of my brother John—he ends the story by saying that the Lone Ranger has to wear a mask because he is sooo ugly, and cross-eyed, too! This makes me feel terrible all over again, but I do not dare to cry with John. They must think that I am brave and grown up. Only Pupa can see me cry, and Maureen.

The next morning is mine—but there is almost no one around to enjoy it with. For they are sleepy and still in bed. Only my tired parents hover about, and Priscilla, I think, and Maureen, and of course the nurses. And every Christmas I get pretty much the same thing: dolls and books. I like dolls, but year after year after year I ask Santa for the Bones Brothers Ranch from the F.A.O. Schwarz catalog. I *am in the middle of a horse phase, and sometimes I do not speak, I only neigh and snort. I trot and canter everywhere and ask people to address me as Gallant Bess. Sometimes I am Misty; sometimes Black Beauty.*

Santa Claus will never bring the Bones Brothers Ranch. Finally, when I am twelve, Priscilla who is also my godmother, and Bill, who is my godfather, buy it for me.

Of course I am too old for it by then—I am already beginning to collect photos of Montgomery Clift. But I appreciate what they have done; I know what they meant.

I take my dolls and books upstairs and put them carefully on my bed. I am very happy. I never think to go downstairs again. I will have my Christmas lunch early, in the breakfast room with Pupa. I play for the rest of the morning in my room with my dolls—I look through the books quickly, flip through the pictures. I give the dolls names—that is the hardest part. Some names don't suit, and I have to start all over again. Then I must introduce them to my other dolls, and soon I am making up stories about them. I instruct the new dolls about how to behave and tell them their roles. Otherwise, they won't fit in and can't be part of my stories. I hear the laughter downstairs and the talk, so much talk, but really it is better up here alone. It is cozier, and it is all my own. And that is how I'm learning to be—more comfortable alone than with the family downstairs.

 *Seven*

*M*y sister Aloise understood. Twenty years my senior, and beginning her own family, she intuited my growing loneliness and understood the damage that isolation does. I often played alone, especially in summertime in Sharon, exploring the vast rooms of our enormous house. Our home there, which looked quite normal from the outside, colonial white clapboard with columned porches, was filled inside with Mexican artifacts, all of them given to my father during the anticlerical revolution, the Spanish court preferring to give away its treasures rather than have them destroyed. There were ornate mantels which had once served as altars, Spanish tiles and urns, the emperor Maximillian's very own desk, and an airy, two-story patio filled with flowering plants and trees and wrought-iron chairs and tables. And every room held treasures for a curious child—lace fans, ivory thimbles, tiny tea sets made of silver, Mexican dolls, silk serapes and mantillas with tortoiseshell combs to secure them. In later years I would make two friends there but when I was a little girl, my Connecticut summers were long and spent on my own.

I believe Aloise knew what it was to feel very much alone in a big family. We used to joke that Allie always looked like the governess in family photos. And indeed she does. She was big for her age, and John, the oldest boy and second child, was quite small, a bright redhead with big freckles and an impish smile—and then there were the others: Priscilla, Jimmy, Jane, Billy, and Patricia. The babies, Reid and Maureen, were too little to sit or stand in most of those photos and had to be held in the nurses' arms. But there stands Allie, towering over the rest, large and round, her straight brown hair razor-cut, her face subdued. Beginning at the level of her chest, six little brothers and sisters standing straight in a row. It doesn't look as though she did much playing herself. Maybe being the oldest precluded play; maybe she felt too responsible or too mature. It is possible that at times she felt more adult than our own mother. I wonder if that is why she had so many children herself, to get it right this time, and to have some play.

What Allie wanted most for her own children was a Norman Rockwell existence; she wanted them to do all the "normal" things that we Buckleys had never done: join the Girl Scouts, play Little League baseball, and live in a community where they could actually see the house next door. In these aspirations she was unmercifully teased by my father. He also found her liberal, "Dr. Spock" attitudes permissive. I relished them and I reveled in the attention and care she gave me.

Allie periodically "kidnapped" me and took me to her home in Florida "to play with Jimmy," her oldest son—the first of *her* ten children. My nephew Jim was six years younger than I, and already I thought of him as my little brother. Allie allowed me to feel grown-up with Jimmy and superior; on the other hand, she provided me a playmate, and after a day or so I regressed happily, and played trucks and fire engines with him, and made sand castles and fished.

Aloise was beautiful. She had enormous blue eyes and thick black lashes, a flared straight nose, and a full, sensual mouth. It was my father's mouth, pure Buckley, and like him, Allie could be cruel. No one could make you feel more foolish than she, no one mock you as adeptly. No one could make you laugh like Aloise, or make others laugh *at* you. I was spared her sarcasm until my adolescence; then I was fair game like everyone else. But when I was a child, oh, my! no one was as magical as she, or provided more fun, more fantasy and play. Allie could make wolf shadows on the wall with her hands; Allie made cats' cradles and origami birds and told ghost stories replete with sound effects, howls and eerie sighs and creaks. And if you fell and bumped your knee on something, Allie spanked the something right then and there, and she made the something cry, too. And apologize and promise never again to bump your knee. I thought my sister Allie was the cat's pajamas.

The other sister who befriended me was Priscilla. Pitts was seventeen years older than I. She took me to movies and for my very first visit to Radio City Music Hall. Once, on my birthday, we went to the Gene Autry Rodeo at Madison Square Garden! Until that moment, seeing Gene Autry's familiar face, I didn't understand that movie stars were actually flesh-and-blood people. There were lots of things I didn't understand and never asked about. I didn't want to look dumb. Not in my family.

Some years later, when Priscilla worked at United Press in Paris, she invited Maureen and me abroad during two consecutive summers. We traveled, and broke down,

*Mother and "the girls": Aloise, Priscilla, Maureen, Aloise Sr., Carol,
Patricia, and Jane (Great Elm, Sharon, Connecticut).*

all over Europe in a 1938 Citroën and learned to eat good
food and even learned a little history. I was, I think, "*impossible.*" That is the worst thing I have ever heard Priscilla
say about anyone or anything. On one trip I refused to take
off my navy blue wool coat, even in the Roman Forum—98
smoldering degrees and no trees for shade. That was because I thought I was fat—and I didn't like the Best &
Company dresses Mother insisted I wear. The next summer
I alternately borrowed Pitts's and Maureen's white sweat-

ers and got them very, very dirty indeed. But that was the point! I was saving my own white sweater for the return voyage.

Jane and Trish were still college girls, attending Smith and Vassar. I remember that they wore loafers and long men's shirts hanging over their shorts. They smoked and seemed to be best friends. I admired them a great deal. Jane had a perfect brown pageboy and Trish, a glinting red one. They both wore bright red lipstick, and Jane even polished her nails to match! They both married soon after college, which was exactly what women were meant to do in those days. Even smart, college-educated women.

"The boys," as Mother called them, were not around much, either still in the service or catching up on their education immediately after. I remember seeing Jim for the first time in Sharon in 1946.

There is such excitement in the house, everyone whispering, everyone telling me to "Shh, don't tell Mother."

Tell Mother what?

"Don't tell Mother," says Reid, "or Jack Frost will come and get you and take you away forever."

"Don't tell Mother what?"

"I won't tell you, because if you know, you'll tell!"

"I hate you," I say to Reid and run to Maureen's room, where she is trying to read.

"Go away."

"Tell Mother what? Tell Mother what?"

"It's a secret," says Maureen. "A family secret."

"But I'm a family, I'm a family too!" I cry. "Tell me, tell me, tell me . . ." I jump up and down, pulling at the spread. Our beds are old-fashioned and very tall. To get into them, I have to be lifted up.

"All right, all right," says Maureen wearily. "But you have to promise. Catholic word of honor. Cross your heart and hope to die."

I cross my heart and hope to die.

"Jimmy is coming home today. From the war." Maureen says this with wonder, whispering in my ear. "And Mother doesn't know. Father is taking her out for a long, long drive—I think he's going to pretend to get lost! And Pitts is driving Jimmy home from his ship in New York, so he'll be here when Mother comes home. And we're all having a big supper in celebration."

"Like a birthday party?"

"Sort of."

"And cake?"

"I guess."

Oh, I am excited. I babble to Pupa when she gives me my bath and when she puts me in my pajamas, "Vamos a tener un birthday party, Felipa, para Jeemee, mi hermano, Jeemee!" I can barely eat my supper for the excitement of it all. I still eat with Felipa, upstairs in the nursery at a yellow-painted table with yellow-painted chairs, gobbling down my scrambled eggs and peas. I have scrambled eggs and peas one night and scrambled hamburger and peas the next. Always peas.

I hear the massive front door open downstairs, and a cry from my mother, and I rush from the table without asking "May I be excused."

"Jimmy! Jimmy," cries Mother and by the time I peek over the banister, she is in the arms of a handsome young man, dressed in a blue-gray uniform. He makes little gulp-noises, and my mother cries and cries. And everyone is standing about them, half smiling, half crying. I don't go down because I am too shy to say hello. I think he is the

*brother who sent me a turtle from the Pacific, the turtle
with an American flag painted on its shell.*

He wore his uniform the next morning, and immediately after breakfast he set off walking across the lawns and up the hill, past the apple orchard, into the woods. My brother Jim had always had a special kinship with nature, and once a fox, a notoriously shy animal, followed him home from the fields. Another time, Jim brought home a flying squirrel, which terrified Mademoiselle and Mother, flying from room to room as they shrieked and chased after it, waving magazines and newspapers. My brother Jimmy was a beautiful shy young man, and I whispered to my friend Buddy Bristol the morning after his return home that I planned to marry him. "He's your brother," she said. "You can't marry your own brother, silly!"

I remember Billy visiting Camden, just back from his infantry base in Texas. He was thin, and I was fascinated by his Adam's apple, which bopped up and down when he spoke. I felt shy with him. My father complained that he drowned his food in ketchup, a habit I think almost everyone develops in the army. He was dating a woman called Gloria of whom, for some reason, sight unseen, everyone disapproved. Billy was more assertive than my other siblings and often engaged my father in conversation as if he were his peer. My father adored it, for in many ways the respect and awe he seemed to elicit from others kept him isolated and apart. Billy also played Artie Shaw on the record player—especially "Indian Love Song." He played it every afternoon when I was taking my nap.

Reid, of course, was at home more often. He was at Millbrook School and I thought him quite full of himself and conceited. Once I overheard him conspiring with his

The family together after the war. Standing: *Jane, Maureen, John, Jim, Patricia, Bill, Priscilla, Carol, Reid.* Seated: *Father, Mother, Aloise's son Jim Heath, Aloise, and Aloise's husband, Ben Heath.*

friends Pete Coley and Dick Bogardus to steal and sell Maureen's bicycle so that they could buy a canoe and boat down the Housatonic. *I told.* Some hours later Reid pulled me down from an apple tree in the orchard where I had fled (I would build a house in the Great Elm orchard almost thirty years later) and administered my first spanking. He pulled down my underpants right in front of Pete and Dick, and for years I blushed whenever I saw them.

56

The only other corporal punishment I remember was a spanking administered by Ben Heath, Aloise's husband. Ben had glossy black hair with a widow's peak, and I was waiting for Aloise to die so that I could marry him. I showed my love one afternoon in Camden by repeatedly kicking him in the shins. I ignored his many requests to stop. At least when Ben spanked me, he did so modestly, *over* my shorts, not under. And so I have forgiven him.

 *Eight*

Where did she go? How did she disappear? The boisterous, impudent little girl who stuck her tongue out at wedding photographers, held court in Spanish, and kicked her beloved brother-in-law in the shins? The seemingly self-sufficient child? Sometime in the ensuing years I would become fat and stop looking directly at the camera. I was conscious of a coolness in my mother's eyes and of my own inadequacies. For certainly I seemed to be different, not really a bona fide member of the family. I was still in grade school, they were "grown-ups"; I was dumb, they were smart.

Every member of my family, including precocious Maureen, knew and understood and talked and breathed politics. Once, in an effort to join in, I made the mistake of saying that I liked Harry Truman's smile better than General Eisenhower's. I was immediately informed that Democrats were the bad guys, and only *some* Republicans, good. Unfortunately I could never quite figure out who was which. I didn't read the newspaper.

Another of my failings—not liking to read. I wouldn't

learn to like reading until Maureen introduced me to Jane
Austen in my twelfth year. I was often teased about this.
Buckleys read.

"I hope you don't turn into an ignoramus," said my
father.

"Or a dope," said John. My clever brother John, now
back from the war, was sometimes nice to me and sometimes not. Father set about bribing me: he offered to pay
me a dollar a book, which was quite a large sum of money.
Some books I skimmed; most I lied about. I got away with
pretending to read for most of the school year until I listed
The Prince and the Porpoise as one of the books I had most
enjoyed.

I lived now in a make-believe world filled with fantasy
heroes and adventures. For love I turned to my pets, especially to my first dog, a splendid Irish setter called Captain.
He was my life and alter ego for the four years of his
existence and the only dog that I have ever been able properly to train. He heeled and stopped and sat and lay down
on command. He retrieved. He never took his eyes off me.
And at night he took over most of the bed and I would
wake up in a little round bunch at his side. Every spring-
time in Camden, the town put on a dog show. I heard
about it on the local radio and called the telephone number
to sign up. Captain and I trained every afternoon after
school; we trained for weeks and weeks. I asked Leslie to
drive me there in the station wagon.

Captain won Best of Breed and Best in Show, and
though no family member was there to share our victory, I
was the proudest child in town. In late May Captain traveled up to Sharon with the horses, and I was allowed to call
him from Camden and "talk" to him. I called one afternoon after school, the day before we were to come up

ourselves. My sister Patricia, home from Vassar for the weekend, answered the phone. "I see him," she said, "running across the lawn." I could see him too in my mind's eye, his beautiful glossy copper coat and the freedom and stretch of his long legs as he galloped across the Great Elm lawns.

Two days later I ran up to the stables the minute the car door opened. My nurse and I had been met at Penn Station by Mr. Cronin, my father's New York chauffeur, and transferred to Grand Central, for the local train. Mr. Bristol met us at the Amenia station and drove us the five miles to Sharon.

"Where's Captain?" I asked. "Where's Captain?"

Usually he bounded down the front steps, a euphoric, wiggling mass, before the car had even come to a stop—he always understood that it was me in the car. He trusted, I believe, that despite our annual separations I would always return to him.

Our groom at that time was a taciturn man, not the kind of person you'd share chewing gum wads with. He looked at me in dismay. "He was in an accident. He was run over, Miss Carol. I'm sorry, I thought you knew, that someone would have told you."

"But where *is* he? Is he at the doctor's? I have to see him, I *have* to. You see, he wants me . . ."

"Oh, he's . . . he's dead, Miss Carol."

My father had had him buried at a farm we owned. He was afraid that if he were buried at Great Elm, I might spend the summer there, at his grave. He was afraid that I might mourn. He was afraid he might have to see me cry.

I don't remember anyone being there, in the big house, when I walked back from the stables, across the grass, stumbling down the flagstone path. That night, though I

60

was much too old—eight or nine maybe—I climbed the stairs to Pupa's room on the creaky third floor and got into her bed and stayed there, sticking to her until dawn. She smelled of Vaseline. Every night Felipa put Vaseline all over her face and neck and arms. I think she believed it might smooth the pockmarks there, the scars of smallpox, which she'd had as a child. Perhaps that was why she never married, why she went into service and lived most of her lifetime with our family.

My father bought her and her two sisters a house in Mexico City. Pupa was very proud of it. She went there on vacations, though I was never told when she would be leaving or when she would come back, and so I cried heartbroken tears whenever she departed. I fight those tears even today, work not to cry at airports, in cars, at the door of my house, when loved ones depart. I fear they will leave forever as, one day, Felipa did.

> Señora Felipa Vilches
> Calle 7, #332
> Colonia Aldana,
> Mexico D.F., Mexico

That was how I addressed the cards and letters. That is where she went or where, in my mind, she disappeared to. It seemed to me that Pupa went away once on vacation and never came back. It seemed to me that one winter Maureen was gone, too. Mademoiselle Bouchex died of cancer in our house in Camden, and it was after that that the series of governesses began, and the grilled cheese sandwiches. And the candy bars. And potato chips, foods to fill the empty places.

 *Nine*

My father and a group of other parents started a one-room school based on the Calvert School tutoring method. The public school system in South Carolina was inadequate, very few of the local children were prepared for anything beyond high school, if that, and so my father simply founded his own school. My father often started schools for his children for the in-between times: in between living in Paris and London, in between semesters at English boarding schools, in between Sharon and Camden. It was not so much that he was snobbish—my New Orleans mother was the social elitist in the family—as that he considered the American system sorely lacking.

At the Calvert School, Miss Bertie Zemp taught English and history and geography, Mrs. McCann taught math and science. There were eleven students in all, ranging from grades one through grade seven. At some point, in my ninth or tenth year, in order that I not miss the fall semester, I was sent to Camden in early September to live with my governess in a hotel until my parents moved south.

A reception at Kamschatka, Camden, South Carolina.

They traveled down after Thanksgiving and after Kamschatka had been opened.

My brothers and sisters all congregated in Sharon for the Thanksgiving holiday. If I felt angry then, or excluded, I don't remember it; I remember instead a gradual moving into myself, a focus within and an increasing apathy toward the things around me. There was no understanding of childhood depression at that time, no perception that children *could* become depressed. It was years later, in my late twenties, that my depression would take on a destructive force and violently erupt—on a Thanksgiving afternoon.

I would travel down to Camden in early September with whatever governess I had at the time, on the Silver Meteor from Pennsylvania Station. It was still parched summer in South Carolina, and I missed the New England fall, the tart cider and the leaf piles to play in. I missed wearing costumes and knocking on doors on dark Halloweens. Halloween isn't made much of in the South, and besides, my governess would never have let me go out at night, even if I had been asked. I missed being a child at home.

The governess and I shared a room at the Court Inn, an old rambling hotel, and stayed there until my parents moved down in early December. We made an odd pair in the hotel dining room, the Frenchwoman and I. At night after dinner, I did my homework in a corner of our bedroom. Sometimes we played Parcheesi. One year I ate nothing but grilled cheese sandwiches, lunch and supper, and even on Thanksgiving Day. It drove Mademoiselle Rolot to distraction.

My grade school summers in Connecticut were livened by two new friends. I was quite happy with them—a different kind of happiness, though, than my brother Bill remembers:

> Summers were seasons of unmitigated pleasure for us in the late 1930s at Sharon, where my Texan father had brought his brood to rest. There was one obsession

shared by almost all of us, which was the horses and the horse shows. . . . In those days in rural New England only the principal arteries connecting the villages were macadamized. The side roads were dirt, so that Sharon was a network of leafy pleasure and opportunity for the horseman. No day went by at our place without two or three hours' wandering about through the woods and pastures, sometimes at full gallop. . . . [We] young riders would rush into the changing rooms and plunge into the pool.

At lunch, those who had chosen to play golf or tennis joined the riders and we would plan the afternoon—though Mademoiselle was there to see to it that no schedule stood in the way of the forty-five minutes required of every one of us for piano practice. There were five pianos in the house and one organ. It was never absolutely clear whether the sound was worse when all pianos were being exercised jointly or when only one of them was being played.

My Great Elm had little music, a couple of elderly horses, and no family to speak of. Instead, I had Ella, Jeff, Sally, Leslie, and Elizabeth, and a new set of alter-parents, the resident white caretaker, Lyndon Bristol, and his wife, Mary. Mr. Bristol and Mary and their four children lived in a house up past the stables and the swimming pool. Some of my happiest memories are of being allowed to have supper with the Bristols. There I ate with the family at the kitchen table. How I loved those casual meals, for my dinners at Great Elm were still taken alone. I sat at a small table in our enormous dining room, often while the big table was being set by Ella and Jeff for the dinner guests who would be joining my parents. In our house, cocktails were served at seven and a formal dinner at eight. At the Bristols', we had supper at six, still in our play clothes or damp bathing suits, and in the kitchen! Once Mary Bristol baked a deep chocolate cake with a foamy white sugar frosting made of Crisco. She showed me the can with the recipe printed right on it.

Kathleen "Buddy" Bristol and Leslie and Elizabeth's daughter, Alma, were my friends. We played house and tag, and blindman's bluff. We swam and splashed in the pool from morning to night until our fingers and toes were wrinkled and waterlogged. We biked up and down the drives, skidding on gravel, scraping our knees and the palms of our hands. Only Buddy and I biked—Alma didn't have a bicycle. Only Buddy and I swam—Alma wasn't allowed.

Occasionally some family grown-up would remember me and I would be summarily removed for a piano or a riding lesson, but in many ways I was a wild child in summertime, free to roam on my own, undisciplined, for no one was exactly in charge of me. An older brother or sister would probably remark, "Carol really ought to learn tennis (golf) (piano)." Then I was taken to the club for tennis or golf instruction. On those occasions, I was re-dressed, elastic bands and bows tied onto my braids, clean shorts with white stripes down the side donned, and iodine put on my scabby knees. The few children my age at the Sharon Country Club wore impeccable whites and seemed impervious to things like poison ivy and sunburn. The club was a tiny one, built exclusively for golfers, mostly elderly golfers, and so there was very little for children to do there, beyond tennis or golf lessons, no games for them, no pool, no swing sets, no parties, no dances. I thought the children

I infrequently met there "stuck-up" and longed to return to Buddy and Alma, to our spontaneous, unsupervised play. They were endless, those days of summer, innocent, innovative—three young girls taking charge of their empty hours, making make-believe, making do.

 *Ten*

I understood by then that my relationship with my mother was different from that of other children, different even from that of my brothers and sisters. But then, my mother *was* different—she didn't cook, didn't cut out paper dolls, didn't braid hair. On the other hand, she didn't lecture or scold, either. The things my mother did do were either funny or very, very serious. Like praying. Mother prayed at the drop of a hat, anywhere, even in public, and expected you to fall on your knees and join her. But though she is most remembered for her faith, an almost childlike and quite intimate relationship she had with God, it is her "thingamajig" confrontations that I remember most.

I really don't believe that she took a toaster on a picnic in Texas. I think my father made that one up. But I did witness a number of thingamajig crises myself. On Sunday nights, "maid's night off," we often had Mexican suppers consisting of my father's favorite foods, the cans and cartons sent up from Texas by my two aunts. Cans required opening, and for opening, you needed, of course, a can opener: "Oh," cried Mother, "I can't stand this terrible opener! It simply won't work." And indeed, the pencil sharpener hanging on the kitchen wall wasn't doing the job. . . .

Mother's mechanical inability became at times perilous. Once, seeking to open a vent, she pulled the emergency cord on the Orient Express and brought it and a hundred startled passengers to a screaming halt. And then there was her problem with French elevators; there, she could often be observed pounding on the glass with an elegantly gloved hand, crying plaintively, *"Monsieur, monsieur, aidez-moi, s'il vous plaît,"* as she sank jerkily from sight. Once, in Camden, she stapled the satin sleeve of her very best dressing gown to her checkbook.

If Mother was best kept out of the kitchen, one also wished that she had been kept out of her car. She drove Ford LTDs, flooding the engines, often leaving on the hand brakes, and always braking with screeching ferocity. You knew Mother had just arrived home from the fumes of burnt rubber—no wonder we needed Walter to rake the ruts out of the drive. All things mechanical foiled her—my mother's many and endearing talents lay only with the animate.

I had a sense always of her "little girlness" and seeming helplessness. I don't know the origins of her behavior or whether my father may have encouraged these helpless airs. For years, cooped up at Great Elm, she had dealt alone with all the crises children generate while my father sailed the seas to make his fortune. And she managed, if not happily, at least competently. When my older brothers and sisters got into trouble, which was often enough—once they turned all the books in the Sharon library upside down, once John shot out the streetlights in front of our gate with his new .22—it was Mother who smoothed over the crises and kept Father from learning of them. There was nothing more chilling than my father's disapproval. You would go to all ends, including barefaced lying, to avoid it.

And so she was strong, my mother, and my brothers and sisters remember her as such. Yet my own earliest memories of Mother are of a pretty butterfly, bright and enchanting—impossible to catch. She was the oldest child of a rather severe Germanic mother and a gentle, charming father. She had two younger sisters, each as ebullient and funny as she. She had a much younger brother and he, like his sisters, immediately put you at ease and made you feel special. Maybe it was being brought up in New Orleans in their generation, or, maybe it was a gene—whatever, the Steiners were a laughing, jolly bunch. Well into her seventies and eighties, my mother would fall onto her hands and knees when greeting a toddler, for she had an instinctive understanding of people and of children and a talent for meeting their needs.

Men especially loved her. Gentlemen in the neighborhood would drop by unexpectedly, or give her their terrible memoirs to read, or lend her books she didn't want. One particularly humorless and self-important retired army colonel who called on her weekly gave her a book he had written and had vanity-published—about horses.

"Oh," she cried gaily when next he came to call, "I couldn't put it down! It was wonderful. I learned so much about horses. Why, I never knew that . . . that when a horse jumps [she's thinking hard now—frowning, actually] . . . well, that his front legs go over the jump just before his back legs. . . . How fascinating, my dear!"

The colonel was pleased. He blushed. So, of course,

did Maureen and I—we blushed to have such a shameless mother. We knew perfectly well that Mother read only Agatha Christie and Ellery Queen, wedging them in between her household duties, her toilette, and her many prayers. For she was always busy, surrounded by other people, by friends, by my older brothers and sisters, and by the servants. I can remember only one private conversation with her and then I took her by surprise.

I was waiting for my friend Martha Kirk to come over to play. I found my mother sitting in a wrought-iron chair on the bricked terrace of Kamschatka. The terrace looked onto a garden bordered with masses of pink and flame-red azaleas. At the far end lay a rather scummy pool filled with water lilies and bloated goldfish. I waded there in the early spring, catching tadpoles in an empty milk bottle. On this early afternoon there was no telephone in Mother's hand, no canceled checks to paste and tote up in the big flat checkbook she used for household expenses, no list of menus to discuss with Sally, no rosary. My mother was simply sitting quiet and alone. She held out her hand. My mother seldom touched me.

"I am thinking," she says, "of my father, your grandfather. You never knew him; few of you children did, because he died long ago."

I stand by her, holding on to her hand, awkward and as still as can be, for if I move or speak I will lose her—she will fly away to do all those busy things she does.

"He was a wonderful man, your grandfather, very short but very dignified, shorter than your grandmother. My mother was a big woman, and she had a temper. So did I." My mother smiles, remembering. . . .

71

"Once, I was naughty, and do you know what she did?"

"No," I whisper.

Mother laughs. "She knew I was vain—I've always been vain, sweetie. Your grandmother put my beautiful hair into tight pigtails and made me go to Mass that way, looking homely, to punish me for my vanity."

"Oh, how awful!" I sympathize so for I am vain, too. But Mother doesn't hear; she is still remembering.

"When my father died—it was sudden, I was on the train, traveling from Austen, where I had been to see your Grandmother B., to New York City. They sent me a wire—the porter brought it to me—and I cried."

My mother crying—my mother sharing with me that she had cried. I am awed—I feel so very, very special. I can't think what to say or how to tell her that, to tell her what I feel.

She sits up suddenly, all smiling distraction again, and looking past me, calls out, "Well, look who's here! Hello, Martha dear!

"Now, girls, run off to play. Have fun." And looking at her watch, my mother cries out, "Goodness—the time!"

I hated Martha Kirk for coming then and intruding and taking me away. I would seldom see Mother alone and quiet like that again, not until many years later when talking no longer mattered.

Once, as a mother myself, in New York, during one of my numerous attempts to stop smoking, I decorated and furnished a dollhouse with my younger daughter, Carol. Her sister, Anne, had just left for Ethel Walker, the boys, Tommy and Buck, were also off at school, and I wanted to give her, my neglected youngest, some time. For like

Mother, I had put my husband first, loved him the most, and let the love that was left trickle down to the children.

Our dollhouse had many rooms. I had bought it at a charity auction for the Convent of the Sacred Heart at Ninety-first Street and Fifth Avenue. Carol and I managed to spend at least twice the cost of the dollhouse on period furniture and parquet flooring, only a little of which buckled under our ministrations. We papered the attic rooms in flowered chintz and furnished them with early American furniture, tiny Hitchcock chairs and painted blanket chests. We made the drawing room downstairs a fussy chinoiserie, with a minute collection of Chinese porcelain vases and jars scattered about the tabletops, and teak armchairs and settees on an Oriental carpet. In a wonderful shop in the East Nineties, on Madison, we found wax replicas of Edwardian dolls. I purchased an Alice in Wonderland with long blond hair and a royal blue velvet dress. I purchased a nanny, uniformed in white, a plump, aproned cook, and a butler with gray whiskers sprouting from his cheeks. There was a little parlormaid holding a tiny dustpan and brush. Carol asked me some weeks later, "Where are the mother and father?"

Where indeed? It was our servants who had constituted my real family, who were always there, consistent, reliable, caring. I identified with them from my earliest years, felt anger and defensiveness when someone mocked my Mexican nurse's attempts at English, or when a New York bus driver was rude to Mademoiselle. I worried and dithered when Ella was out of sorts, or Jeff, intoxicated. I was later to take up social work as a profession. It had begun there in my childhood, the identification I felt with outsiders and with those less fortunate. My Roman Catholic teachers would complete the job, for along with their rigid explications of church dogma and ritual, the nuns conveyed the universal Christ and the (almost unattainable) concept of love without condition. They were not stingy or selective about love, as many Christians seem to be.

 *Eleven*

I joined the grown-ups at table in my eleventh and twelfth years. In a period of just over three years, from 1949 to 1951, John had married Ann Harding, Jim married Ann Cooley, Jane married Bill Smith, Bill married Patricia Taylor, Trish married Brent Bozell, and my brother Reid married Elizabeth Howell. They began their careers and the process of bearing children—fifty grandchildren in all we would produce—and my sister Priscilla, who didn't marry, moved to Paris to work as a journalist for United Press.

John had joined my father's business, and Jim, having graduated from Yale Law School, would soon join the company as well. Bill, who graduated from Yale in 1951, had also just finished a book, *God and Man at Yale*. I don't think any of us were prepared for the uproar it was to cause, or the celebrity that came fast on its heels. Reid, also at Yale, would begin his officer's training for a stint in the air force and begin the writing his first novel, *Eye of the Hurricane*.

Allie and Ben now lived in Hartford; Jane and her

husband, Bill Smith, in Calgary, Canada; and Trish and Brent in Palo Alto. John and Jim commuted between the Lakeville-Sharon area and New York, and Pat and Bill settled in Stamford and Manhattan. Ella had only one table to set for meals now, and my parents, when they were not entertaining guests, were left with me and Maureen for

With the grown-ups at last, in June 1949. Standing: Bill; his wife, Patricia Taylor; Jim; Reid; Priscilla; Jane's husband, Bill Smith; Patricia; her husband, Brent Bozell. Seated: John's wife, Ann Harding; John; Maureen; Father; Carol; Mother; Allie; Ben Heath; Jane; and Brent's mother, Mrs. Bozell.

company during school holidays. For now I too had been sent to boarding school. "Noroton-on-the-Sound," they called it, a great Georgian mansion built on a point on Connecticut's North Shore, a strict Catholic boarding school for wealthy girls.

My feckless, lazy days had come to a halt. Buddy and Alma and I stopped playing together when I came home on vacation. Sometimes I would look up near the stables, or past the tennis court, and see them talking or see them walk out the gates together and head for town. That amazed me, seeing them stroll out the Great Elm gates like that—so free! I don't know exactly how it happened, how I let our friendship lapse. Perhaps there was some sort of tacit understanding between our parents, or perhaps I was a snotty, snobby, self-absorbed adolescent. If I was, I was also a terribly lonely one.

The Sacred Heart order had been founded during the French Revolution by Saint Madeleine Sophie Barat, a visionary woman who promoted the outlandish belief that young women of good family deserved as fine an education as their male counterparts. The mothers were often referred to as the Mesdames du Sacre Coeur, an appellation repugnant to them for sounding exclusive and snobbish. They preferred to be called instead "the religious of the Sacred Heart."

We are lined up in the dormitory. We have unpacked our uniforms: gray wool jumpers with name tags, white cotton blouses with name tags, gray knee socks, and two pairs of brown oxfords. Our stunning gym clothes have yet to be handed out: large blue bloomers with a matching blue tunic affair that reaches down to our knees. We have different white shirts for gym and they are perpetually sweat-

rimmed and smelly. Only our flannel pajamas and our bathrobes vary, show that we have come from other places. I have two identical pairs of pajamas with pink roses on them (and name tags) and two pairs with blue roses. They have elastic at the wrists and ankles. I look like a clown in my bedclothes; some of the girls look like scarecrows. We are either short and plump or tall and skinny. We are twelve and thirteen years old. We are scared witless.

We have been delivered that afternoon in limousines and station wagons. Most of us have never been away from home. The very rich don't go to camp; they go to their summer places. Some of the girls have attended Sacred Heart primary schools—especially the girls from Grosse Pointe. They are not as awed as the rest of us by these black-robed women with the jingling rosaries at their waists. We number about ten. We all act a little stunned. Our parents have left right away—the nuns wanted it that way. Our parents tell us later that they cried in their cars all the way home—Mother said Maureen cried too.

We don't cry yet. We don't know about homesickness. We don't have words for that ominous, scared feeling in our chests. We have already learned to curtsy when passing a nun in the halls, and to say "Mother" when addressing one. I slip up—I say a southern "ma'am." Everyone giggles at that. We are told about the rule of silence: no speaking in the dormitory, no speaking in the halls, no speaking in the classrooms, no speaking in the chapel. We speak at meals, after the bell has rung, which is after grace, after the reading, and after the announcements. At that point we have all begun to stuff our mouths, so we talk as fast as we can, spitting crumbs and dribbles of milk. Patsy McCann puts her pink plastic retainer in a paper napkin and throws it away by mistake. We all have to search the garbage for

Patsy's retainer. We do this for the next two years—look for Patsy McCann's retainer in the trash can after meals.

We are lined up in front of our white-curtained booths. Within each is a small bed, white covers, a very small chest of drawers, and a straight chair. We listen intently as Mother continues to explain the rules. There are so many to remember! We are much too intimidated to break them, at least until third or fourth academic (junior and senior year). We have all been well, and strictly, brought up. We do as we are told. These are the 1950s. Eisenhower is president. The world is safe, except for the Communists. Our country and our parents are right in all matters, just as right as the pope and our parish priest and, now, the Sacred Heart nuns. It almost makes you feel important to think that there are so many people put on earth just to tell you what is right. And wrong.

The older girls look smug and somewhat condescending. They sleep in actual bedrooms, four to a room. They seem happy to be here and greet each other with hugs and calls. Some of them wear green ribbons, some blue. These are the important girls—they are student government.

On the first night, Mother tells us that we will rise at six—Mass at seven. Six A.M.! Up? She shows us how to make our beds with hospital corners. I spend the night in panic—I have never made a bed before. I am frantic, and toss and turn. For years to come, learning new tasks will agitate me. Because I will definitely fail—I will do it wrong, and then people will know the truth about me: that I am stupid and clumsy. I am neither, and for four brief years, as the nuns give me more and more responsibility—in my senior year I am president of the school, sashaying about with my own self-important blue ribbon—they work to give me some belief in myself, to give me confidence.

Mother Heide is our theology teacher. She has a white Byzantine face and comes from a Chicago candy-fortune family. She gives us our first quiz. We all fail! She gives it to us a second time. We all get a hundred. And so we learn to learn. We study logic, theology (Catholic), philosophy (mostly Catholic except for the Greeks), history (quite Catholic in that we learn nothing of the Spanish Inquisition or of the Medici popes), Latin (church pronunciation), and English literature.

The days passed quickly at Noroton, quickly and also unbearably slowly. We were only allowed home on the major holidays, and once a month permitted out for Sunday lunch. My brother Bill and his wife, Pat, who had a home on Wallach's Point in Stamford—I could see their house across the water—often invited me for Sunday lunch. They were elegant and lively, amusing, worldly—everything I wanted to be someday and didn't quite feel like, with my spotty face and dull gray uniform. Pat was a daunting beauty, tall, glamorous, but Bill was still just my brother Billy, a little smarter than most, but Billy nonetheless, generous and affectionate.

On our one winter weekend off campus, Maureen invited me to stay with her at Smith College. I had my first pizza there in Northampton, went to my first drive-in movie, had my first introduction to the closeness and camaraderie of adult women. I took her friends as my own, acted as grown up as I could, and reveled in their kind attentions. After all, what was Maureen's was also mine, and she allowed me to believe that.

Returning to the confines of Noroton after my visits to Maureen left me sad. I also yearned for the wonderful freedom of college life, though I had been well indoctrinated by my mentors—only a Catholic college would do for me. The Sacred Heart nuns took their vocations seriously: to prepare us for our place in life, to teach us to be good wives and mothers, good Catholic women. Women were still to marry and stay at home; professions and careers were for the single woman, a kind of second-best option, work for idle hands.

The nuns themselves came from affluent backgrounds, were college-educated women, and so in some ways they were familiar, in other ways mysterious and foreign. They had apparently no bodily functions; they never ate or drank in our presence, they never seemed to blow their noses, or cough; they didn't even walk—they wafted, black robes swirling at the tiny polished boots they wore, which miraculously never made a sound as they slipped in and out of rooms and up and down the corridors. And on Sunday afternoons, at Benediction, they lifted their sweet voices in unison, kneeling in adoration of the Host—why, it gave you the shivers, it made you know absolutely the presence of God (and fear Him a little, too).

We learned good diction and posture and curtsying at Noroton, and also to sew. I lied once and said I'd lost my apron (the one I'd been not sewing on). Walking though the front hall one afternoon, my sewing teacher, the awesome Mother Fox, swooped down and grabbed my chin, and hissed: "You may fool the others, Miss Buckley, but I have your number." Oh, God! Every spring in her long black robes, long, lean Mother Genevieve Fox placed ladders against the majestic trees and, climbing much higher than I ever would dare, found the abhorrent crows' nests and cut off the heads of the baby crows! With secateurs. So the songbirds would come . . .

There was some pretense in those days at teaching

girls math and science, but those subjects were given low priority. In second academic, we came across a new nun, a mother, who walked outside on the lawn saying her rosary and who weeded the walks. Mothers didn't usually do manual labor—the sisters did that. The following year, she became third academic science teacher. We were terrible to her. Like the little animals we were, we scented her vulnerability. Patsy McCann painted a lipsticked mouth and mascaraed eyelashes on an amoeba on the board. She did this behind Mother's back. We exploded with laughter. Mother began to weep and fled the room. We never saw her again. We had given her her second nervous breakdown—we were vicious little girls, nasty, coating our behavior with piety.

We were also "good" girls, idealistic; we believed, we prayed. Every Easter during Holy Week, the heartwrenching liturgy convinced two or three of us that we had vocations. But not me. Never once did I think I had a vocation. Even then, I understood at least some truths about myself, about my appetites and sloth. My mentor, Reverend Mother Coakley, a beautiful young woman, gentle and delicate, had aspirations for me. She hoped that I would become a great Catholic writer. How I loved her! How I wanted to be what she wanted me to be. How I would fail her, for what she gave me, the confidence she had in me, the caring, came too late to assuage my child's appetite and my childish needs.

If I achieved any maturity before leaving home to marry, it came at the hands of the Sacred Heart nuns. And while I spent at least two of my four years at the convent school in Noroton, Connecticut, feeling intimidated and anxious, I nevertheless acquired most of the basic skills that children are meant to learn at home. I also learned to examine my conscience nightly and to acknowledge my sinfulness. You had simply to *be* a Roman Catholic in the 1950s to sin; even *thoughts* were sinful in those days, mean thoughts, angry thoughts, and of course the very worst of all, *lustful* thoughts. Yet despite my continuing unworthiness, under the strict but benevolent tutelage of the nuns, I began to have some inkling that I was capable and bright and, on most occasions, responsible.

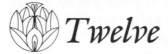 *Twelve*

*I*t was at this time, during the early 1950s, that my parents engaged in the Great Hay Fever Escape. Father had developed high blood pressure, and his doctor prescribed trips abroad in order to avoid the spores and pollens that abounded in Sharon, Connecticut, and set him sniffling and sneezing from May to September. Maureen and I, the only two children left at home, accompanied him and Mother, and sometimes Mr. Bristol and the Cadillac, on their summer sojourns to Europe.

My father had a healthy respect for all modern contraptions and refused to fly and so our voyages abroad were taken aboard the Cunard *Queen*s and, after it was launched, on the stately *United States* (because it was American and all things American were good, were *best*).

They were wonderful trips for a starstruck child like me because we traveled first class and so did the movie stars! They were wonderful trips as well because, for a period of two or three years during my early adolescence, I had my parents near. No sooner had we settled into our staterooms and read the cards on the bon voyage baskets of fruit, the bottles of champagne and bouquets of flowers, than I hurried to read the passenger list: Mr. and Mrs. Clark Gable, Mr. and Mrs. Gary Cooper, Miss Ginger Rogers. . . . Once at the Lancaster Hotel in Paris, a very discreet small hotel just off the Champs-Élysées, I rode upstairs in a tiny glass elevator with Hedy Lamarr. Just me and Hedy. She wore a leopard coat.

Packing was an enormous project and took Mother and her personal maid Elizabeth most of the month of May. Steamer trunks were packed with garments carefully folded in tissue paper. There were shoe cases with satin linings and hatboxes, and the special suitcase reserved for American toilet paper—the paper abroad having the consistency and absorbency of cardboard. Maureen and I packed in jumbles, often the night before, and our wardrobes showed it, a fact that Mother never hesitated to let us know. How one looked and presented oneself was very important to her.

We drove in the limousine, with Bristol, Leslie, and the bags following in one of the station wagons, down old Route 22 to the Saw Mill River Parkway and down the Hudson to the piers. How your heart jumped to spot the first majestic funnels of the ship! Sometimes there were two and three stately ocean liners moored at dock. Often friends had assembled for a bon voyage party and the docks were a jumble of passengers, guests, porters, and Meyer Davis orchestras piping us aboard. There was confetti, there were balloons and elegant ship's officers directing passengers to decks and cabins, stewards and stewardesses introducing themselves, offering help. There was nothing you couldn't command at the ring of a bell. The stewardess

would even take up a hem if you had ripped it. Often
Maureen and I arrived on board with dresses too long or
hems already bunched and coming loose.

My parents' stateroom was filled with guests and
wrapped baskets of goodies and popping bottles of champagne. Mr. and Mrs. Smith were there, he an old renegade
oilman, she a dithery, gracious lady given to mink coats
and Communist affiliation. Father had never quite forgiven
Warren Smith for becoming a Venezuelan citizen. In my
father's eyes, giving up your citizenship was akin to leaving
the church—and not even a graduated income tax could
justify it. There was also Father's business associate, Mr.
Montgomery, and his wooden leg, an appendage that was
only alluded to in whispers and which I therefore found
fascinating. The Miss Hembdts, Father's two secretaries,
were sometimes there, Baron and Mrs. de Lustrac, old
friends from their Paris days, the Fergie Reids, and who
else? They were interchangeable, my parents' old friends,
gray-haired, gray-faced, and as far as I was concerned,
bor-ing. Maureen and I would slip away and stand on
deck, watching the tourist-class passengers board, watching the young people—students, tourists, girls and boys
our own ages.

*I live now in a perpetual state of "in-loveness." First there
was the Lone Ranger, then Aloise's husband, Ben Heath,
and then Montgomery Clift; now almost anyone would do,
but there seems to be no one under fifty traveling first class.
Except the ship's officers.*

*"I like the one who does the bingo. Don't you think
he's cute, Maureen?"*

" 'Cute,' ugh."

"All right, handsome, then."

"*Carol, it's breakfast time. Please, I can't deal with your crushes this early in the morning.*"

"*You just fall in love with book heroes like the Scarlet Pimpernel and Rhett Butler.*"

"*I fall in love with book writers, like Joseph Conrad, like Henry James. I don't read* The Scarlet Pimpernel, *I don't read Margaret Mitchell . . .*"

"*Who's Margaret Mitchell?*"

"*Oh, Carol . . . Carol!*"

I know enough to be quiet; I know I've said something stupid, which I am. We are in bed in our pajamas, in our stateroom, with trays—little fat pots of coffee, pitchers of hot milk, triangles of toast with strawberry jam. I sneak a look at Maureen. She has soft brown hair in a pageboy at her shoulders. She has her nose in a book—always in a book! Maureen has a long nose, she has a Buckley nose; mine is slender and straight like Mother's. I think I am prettier than Maureen—not smarter, but prettier. Maybe that's why I'm after boys and she's not. Because there is so much more going on in her head.

"*Maureen?*"

"*Yes?*"

"*Will you play Ping-Pong with me?*"

"*Yes.*"

We dress warmly; the Atlantic is cold even in summer, and on deck the wind always blows, salty and brisk. My mother and father walk the deck each morning, she in her high heels, with a little scarf tied around her head to keep her careful curls in place. He wears his hat, so my father walks the decks with one hand raised, holding tight to his hat to keep it from flying off. I wonder why he wears it at all. After Ping-Pong, a steward walks about ringing the bell for "elevenses," steaming hot mugs of bouillon, which are served at your deck chair. We lie there, heavy, stiff blankets pulled up to our necks. My ship's officer is nowhere to be found and so I close my eyes and daydream. Rhett Butler will do just fine.

After lunch there is the movie, after the movie, cards or bingo and tea, tiny sandwiches with watercress and sliced cucumbers, and iced cakes and pastries. After that, we return to our cabins to "rest." Changing for dinner is an elaborate ritual. Our dresses must be different for every night, and our shoes, most often satin, must match, and our evening purses, tiny little sacks and envelopes embroidered with sequins or seed pearls. Then there is the jewelry; it matches, too—pearls with pearls, sapphires and diamonds with sapphires and diamonds. Don't mix platinum and gold, don't even think of wearing silver, don't mix emeralds with rubies, don't wear semiprecious stones unless they are very, very big—eye-popping big.

I am thirteen years old, maybe fourteen. I know all these things, I have all these things, the evening dresses and matching shoes, the jewelry, the silk purses. What I don't have is much sense and what I don't know is what is wrong with me, why I have this powerful longing, why I want so. I don't know about being a teenager, I don't know about sex, I don't even know about my own body. When I menstruated, I was sent home from school. That year's governess put me in the bathtub and procured a belt and Kotex and left me alone with them to figure it out.

"Maureen?"

"Yes?"

"Do you think Bob Hope will be in the dining room?"

"I think he will, Carol, but please pretend not to look. I mean, don't stare."

*"Maureen? Do you think anyone will ever ask me to
dance? Do you think I'll ever have a boyfriend?"*

*Maureen looks over at me, looks over my shoulder at
the mirror I am primping before. She smiles. She says from
behind me, "Yes, Carol, I promise—you will someday have
a boyfriend. You're very pretty, you know."*

*I clip on my tiny pearl earrings. I feel all warm and
happy.*

*"Maureen, can I borrow your white pumps? I don't
want to get mine dirty, and maybe tonight he'll ask me to
dance."*

Most often, after a staid six days aboard ship, we
disembarked in Le Havre, and there all Anglo order vanished, blue-smocked French porters expostulating and
shoving, bags and bundles snatched and disappeared until
miraculously everything was reunited aboard the Boat
Train to Paris. In the early 1950s Europe was still in recovery from the Second World War. Porters, cabdrivers,
guides, competed ferociously for a chance at the American
dollar, and in the countryside, children of nine and ten
carried bags, gardened, and worked in sculleries. Americans were kings then, open-handed conquerors.

We stayed in the same suite of rooms at the Lancaster
and dined out regularly at the Vert Gallant, at the Tour
D'Argent, famous for its pressed duck. Sometimes we went
to Les Halles, the market, for onion soup smothered in
cheese, but we were almost always too early to see the
"real" people. For that you had to stay awake until three
and four in the morning. It was the in thing for American
tourists to do, to walk over to Les Halles a bit tipsy, after
a nightclub or two, and share hot bread and soup with the

truck drivers and farmers who had driven in from the countryside. Our parents were older and we were always in bed by eleven.

We visited the Louvre and Versailles. We shopped for perfume and silk and chiffon scarves that we would never wear. We bought kid gloves in all colors. Mother visited the House of Jean Patou and had a most elaborate and unflattering evening dress designed. When my father made no comment, in fact didn't even notice, she burst into tears. Maureen gave him a lecture, told him what for—Maureen was honest always and sometimes quite stern.

She and I were losing patience with our parents. They embarrassed us, for we shared that exquisite teenage sensitivity to drawing the attention of others. Sometimes, after tasting it, Father actually sent the wine back. Misery! On the other hand, our parents were never boring. The very interplay of their two personalities and the need and love they retained for each other was a rarity, something I seldom perceived in the parents of my friends. The energy between my parents never diminished. It was a love that one yearned to find for oneself, but it was also hard to penetrate, to share in.

In Spain, the summer of '52, our car had an *I* license, standing for "international," but the Spanish interpreted it as *I* for Italy and booed and mocked us for our cowardice during the war. When Mother discovered this, she insisted on placing an American flag on the aerial. This, coupled with her habit of throwing candies out the window whenever we passed a group of children had Maureen and me blushing and cringing in the back seat.

One morning in Málaga, Father decided arbitrarily that we must be constipated and forced us to eat fresh figs and All-Bran for every breakfast no matter how much we

My parents, Will and Aloise Buckley, in South Carolina, Easter 1945.

protested or raced each other to the bathroom. My father
was given to health kicks. There was a whole winter in
Camden, I remember, being force-fed blackstrap molasses
and wheat germ. Then there were the pills that tasted of
fish oil. Maureen and I retaliated for the All-Bran by "sight-
ing" ragweed along the roads, hoping to induce a bad case
of the dread hay fever.

Maureen had hiccups in Estoril—three days of them,
probably caused by All-Bran effusion—and my father
wrote a dummy letter in Portuguese allegedly from the
hotel manager and slipped it under our door. The letter
stated his concern and embarrassment at her condition of
chronic "hiccupos," and suggested we might find alternate

accommodations if they continued. Maureen was nineteen years old and indignant that Father would think her so stupid as to believe his practical jokes. I was outraged too, for I had all the pretensions of an adult woman.

We had tea with the deposed Italian king, Umberto II. That seemed to be what King Umberto did, entertain American tourists for tea. I wore orange lipstick with a pink piquet dress, and Mother made me wipe it off. I was furious with her, insulted, and also very disappointed with the king, a rather somber man in somber clothes. No crown, no retinue . . .

In the evenings, we played canasta, my father and I pairing up against Maureen and Mother. Our team won consistently. I liked that; it made me feel confident, having a father who enjoyed me and wanted me on his team.

Father had his first stroke when I was fifteen. After that, they traveled summers to Badgastein to take the waters and mineral baths—my mother believed they would help his paralysis. The trips were taken with male attendants and nurses and, occasionally, a long-suffering Maureen. I don't think my mother had the energy to deal with a pouty teenager. My father's illness consumed her.

I spent the summers of my late adolescence parentless, an endless succession of sunlit days by myself: week after week of empty, yearning Sharon days . . . yearning for what I did not know. They were days of mourning, but I did not understand that then. My achievements at school seemed not to count for much. I had been performing for "them," after all, for the family—to have them notice me and be proud. But how could they notice when we were a family on hold, preoccupied, a family waiting for the final loss of the paralyzed man who had so dominated our lives?

My father, the man I knew to be my father, was gone,

changed irrevocably. His speech was slurred, and his face, devoid of expression, seemed masklike. Sometimes even his eyes were too tired to move, and he stared blankly at nothing. And my mother, still youthful in her early sixties, gave what she had to give completely to him, simply loved him without reservation. At a time when we might have grown closer, for our summers abroad had begun to bring us together, we had begun to laugh together even as she and Maureen and I competed for my father's attention. But now my mother's heart and energy were consumed by him and by his tragic deterioration. Each stroke took away another part of him.

I spent the summer months daydreaming, a self-conscious, self-preoccupied half-child, half-woman, catered to by servants in a kind of opulent neglect. Sometimes I would have a Noroton friend visit, sometimes I visited a friend. In Sharon I hung out with my nephew Jim, going to movies, swimming at the pool. On weekends, things livened as members of the family congregated at the big house for dinner—Ann and John from Lakeville, Jim and Ann from Sharon, and Priscilla from the city. But during the week I had dinner with my sister Aloise, who spent her summers in a house at Great Elm. It was a renovated barn big enough to accommodate her eight children and a nurse and cook. There were two more children still to come.

> A happy, happy valentine
> To the mother of my lovely nine.
> Love, Ben
> Caracas, Venezuela
>
> Will you still love me, darling Ben,
> When I tell you it is ten?

93

Love, Allie
Hartford, Connecticut

Allie and Ben now lived in West Hartford, Ben commuting to New York City, where he worked in my father's company. In the summer, with his family in Sharon at Great Elm, Ben stayed in New York and came out only on weekends. I think Allie was lonely and happy in the evening to give over the care of her children to their nurse and to come down to the relative peace of the big house for dinner. One summer we watched the McCarthy hearings on a staticky black-and-white television; one heavy, humid summer night, eating outdoors on the terrace, we heard the execution of Julius and Ethel Rosenberg on the radio, this eerie experience as the electric bug light snapped and crackled in the dark.

I felt grown-up to be with her, grown-up to be allowed to drink and smoke in her presence. I was fifteen years old, too young to do either, but Allie was permissive and liked bending the rules. Often after dinner, working on a needle-point Christmas stocking for one of her children or hooking a nursery-rhyme rug for the nursery, she talked. She talked as if I were an adult, talked of things she shouldn't have, things I wasn't old enough to know or understand. She analyzed the marriages and personalities of my brothers and sisters, often mocked their husbands and wives and mimicked their children, always with such wit and cleverness that you were compelled to laugh in response. Sometimes, though, when she spoke of my father, she spoke angrily, defending against her own grief with sarcasm and pretend indifference. Aloise had a different father, a more powerful and perhaps more intrusive one, not the accepting, gentle, if remote, man I knew.

94

"Dinner must have been early on those evenings," she wrote, "for in memory, the sun glints strongly through the heavy elms beyond the western windows, and a curtain is always being drawn, or a blind lowered, in order to present a child with a clearer and more comfortable view of his unfinished tuna fish on toast. There are no guests on these occasions, which is the reason Aloise and John and Priscilla and Jimmy and Mademoiselle are having dinner in the upper dining room with Mama and Papa. Jane, Billy, and Patricia, too young to be so honored, are at their own table in the lower dining room, happily not eating their vegetables, because Mexican Nana, *their* supervisor, has her meals in the kitchen. Reid, Maureen, and Carol are placidly unborn. . . .

"At the foot of the table sits Papa, eating, talking, laughing, teasing, dominating the table with gusto and vigor, the gaiety and the concentration on the moment at hand which, until his last illness, entered the house and left it only with him. (Only when he turns to Mademoiselle does his manner change to the grave and slightly puzzled courtesy with which he treats all plain women: Father's 'What *can* God have been thinking of?' expression, his daughters called it many years later.)"

In the same piece, written shortly after Father's death, Allie says: "Aloise sits next to Mama, because Aloise is both plain and argumentative and Papa, often articulately, deplores these characteristics in any female of any age."

Aloise was trapped by her own ambivalence, irrevocably bound to the family by her position as firstborn, even to emulating my mother by having ten children of her own. On the other hand, she was not my mother; she had my father's mind, brilliant and analytic, and she was a wonderfully talented writer—all this subsumed in domesticity and motherhood. She now wrote once or twice a year, *maybe*—and that had to be dragged from her. She composed elaborate poems for birthdays and celebrations, finishing them up on long yellow legal pads, often just minutes before the cake was cut and candles blown. She also wrote an annual Christmas story for Bill's new magazine, *National Review,* an endeavor that had Priscilla and Bill on the phone to her day after day, prodding, imploring, and the printers going wild with exasperation. Her procrastination had to do with her perfectionism and with never producing anything that was *quite* good enough. What would you expect from a brilliant and beautiful woman who saw herself only as "plain and argumentative"? Our father asked only one thing of his children, say my brothers and sisters: "that they be absolutely perfect."

We are in the old playroom downstairs, away from the rooms the family uses now, away from the library with the Spanish tiles and dark Mexican oak. She has the radio on, but we do not listen, my sister and I, the oldest and youngest children of the family. I am fifteen. She is thirty-five, already looking middle-aged, hair graying, winged back from her dramatic widow's peak, luminous eyes, a set mouth with the lipstick bitten off, a Camel lit in the ashtray by her side, a glass of vodka. Aloise works at the needlepoint in her lap; she does not look at me, her hands move up and down in steady rhythm, stopping only to reach for the cigarette, to lift the glass to her lips.

"He liked it when you were brave, you always had to be brave in front of Father."

She is speaking of my father in the past tense as if he is dead, but he is not, he is taking the waters in Badgastein.

"When I broke my arm, when it set wrong, Dr. Chaffee came to the house."

"How old were you?" I ask. It is important for me to know, to make my brothers and sisters into the children they must once have been.

"Eleven. I was eleven.

"They took me to the bathroom off the step-down room—the one that used to be next to your nursery—and Nana opened up the ironing board. They put me on it, they broke my arm again, and Dr. Chaffee set it in a cast." She does not change her expression or her tone of voice. She looks up at me from the work she is doing, looks up quickly, smiles, and looks away.

"Oh, Allie! Without anything? They broke your arm without giving you anything? Oh, it must have hurt so much!"

"Yes, but I didn't cry, I didn't even change my expression, and he was pleased. Father smiled."

Aloise doesn't cry, Aloise doesn't show grief—not until the second stroke, in the winter of 1956, and in my parents' bedroom in Camden, my father talking nonsense, gibberish, making no sense, Aloise cries out like a wounded animal, "Father, Father, Father . . ."

Suppers I had with Allie, days I spent in the big house with Ella and Jeff and Sally and Margaret, our new maid, and with the Carloses up in the apartment over the laundry, and the Bristols in the caretaker's house, and Boykin Williams in the groom's apartment. Boykin was a taciturn man, an alcoholic, often in pain from the broken back he had sustained from a bad fall while training racehorses. He was, I believe, a distant cousin of Ella's. He was bitter at the comedown of having to groom a couple of tired old hunters and to teach a most reluctant me to ride. But he did, with extraordinary patience and diligence—Boykin never let me off the hook. He simply refused to accept any of my excuses: headaches wouldn't do, social engagements, sunburns, poison ivy. "Get up on the horse, Miss Carol," he'd say, and stare at me impassively until I did as I was told. Two years after Boykin's arrival and fourteen harrowing falls later, I had actually learned to jump and to hunt.

So sometimes, when he was sober enough, Boykin and I went riding, but mostly I lounged by the pool, working on my tan with a melanoma-causing mixture of iodine and baby oil, reading novels, and dieting. I also learned to wear high heels, put on makeup, pad my bra, drink coffee, and to smoke Chesterfields and drink beer. All of that took practice. It was what I thought they meant by "growing up."

Thirteen

*A*t seventeen, I thought that becoming an adult meant finding a man of my own to marry—and having babies. Wasn't that what my mother had done? And my sisters? Aloise would have ten children, Jane, six; Patricia, ten; and Maureen, five—often in as many years. During the 1950s when the family congregated at Great Elm on week-ends, there would be as many as two or three pregnant women at the table at one time. My four sisters-in-law joined in the spirit and produced another fourteen grand-children among them. For despite my father's emphasis on education, on literacy and eloquence and political activism, the women in my family were to marry first—marry and multiply. It was only my sister, Priscilla, in choosing not to marry, who made a career for herself as a journalist. And so, though I was certainly expected to finish college, my future entailed marriage, the protection and support of a man, and the raising of children. But first I had to find *him*.

The man in my life, the one whose eyes had lit up when I entered the room, sat confined now in a wheelchair. Three times my brothers and sisters and I had congregated at hospitals to prepare for his death. Three times he had survived, and each time there was a little less of him left. I needed my father, and turned away from his sickness and paralysis, and looked for someone to replace him. And the men I found were always somewhat like him—alone kind of men, moody men locked into their shyness.

I prayed for my father at home and prayed for him at Noroton—the whole school asked to pray for him by Reverend Mother Coakley. We prayed together that he would live to see me graduate. He did. He came in his wheelchair, and the tears rolled down his cheeks.

The following year my father died, October 8, 1958. He fell sick aboard ship, just a few hours out of New York Harbor. My brother Bill went out by tugboat to be with Mother. Father died five days later at Lenox Hill Hospital. That week, on the train to Camden where he was to be buried, a porter whom we had known for many years approached my grieving mother in the club car. "Oh, Miz Buckley," he said, "I is so sorry to see that Mr. Buckley's travelin' down with us in the baggage car. He sure was what I call a fine gentleman!"

I don't remember feeling much by then, not grief, not mourning. I had lost my father during the years of his illness, turned my back, and found another man. About one a month. I was obsessed—"boy-crazy" was the term we used—and as soon as I conquered, I lost interest. For who would want to join a country club that accepted a member like me? And who, on truly knowing me, could love me? And so my conquests were based on a kind of fraudulence, a false, needy me, working constantly to please and seduce.

My two years at Manhattanville College were spent chasing boys, partying on weekends, and playing Scrabble in the school cafeteria. In my sophomore year, I cut final exams. Why not? Who cared? My father's illness and death absorbed us.

My mother was devastated. She was lonely in Sharon and lonely in Camden; she wept. My older sisters were particularly attentive, bringing their children south for long visits, spending time with her at Great Elm. There, in the summer, she had Allie and her ten children and Priscilla on weekends. Pitts had returned to the states from Paris and was now managing editor of *National Review*. John and Ann and Jim and Ann lived nearby. Patricia and Brent had moved to northern Virginia; Reid and his wife, Betsy, lived in Madrid; and Maureen, newly married, lived in New York City with her husband Gerry.

While I was enchanted by my new brother-in-law, Gerry, their marriage in 1958, just months before my father died, took me by surprise, took most of us by surprise, for up to that time Maureen had seemed impervious to romance, a feminist before her time, stubborn, independent, and quite dismissive of the men who courted her, a series of rather drab intellectuals—"pointy heads," as intense as they were humorless.

"Pets," writes my brother Reid in a letter to Maureen and Gerry's five children. "What am I to tell you about your mother? . . . Let me leave you with a deep summer night, in Sharon, when your Aunt Betsy and I gave a hayride and invited a number of our friends, including a young man Maureenie had brought visiting a fortnight before. His name was Gerry O'Reilly. Nice-looking person. Good sense of humor.

" 'Reid,' Aunt Betsy said to me, 'do you see what I see—is that your sister, is that *Maureen*, holding *hands*?'

"Maureen, so jocularly indifferent to the tender passion? Maureen: possibly in love? There were many stars that night; there was even a big balloon of a moon. The scent of hay lay thick on us. We were winding through the White Hollow Road, a dark tunnel between ghostly trees. Who pushed Gerry and Maureen off the wagon? Who urged the driver to hurry along and leave them to walk together? I don't really recall. Probably your parents connived in our connivance. I know only that we left them on that winding road between blackly silhouetted trees, under the flung splendor of the heavens, and that this night every grace and mercy fell upon your mother and father, and the heavens poured on my sister a happiness that was consolidated in you, her children."

Gerry came into her life like a sunburst, an Irish Catholic brought up in Brooklyn, a Notre Dame graduate, a humorous, warm, affectionate man who swept Maureen up and carried her away.

My happiness for them was tempered only by the loss I felt, by the understanding that someone was now closer to Maureen than I, and that my ever-available sister now belonged with someone else. I remember throwing rice at the limousine that drove them away down the Great Elm drive. I remember the catch in my throat, and I remember driving with my date across the state line to a bar in Amenia, New York, and getting very drunk.

During Father's final illness, my mother had come more and more to rely upon her daughters, her adult daughters. At me, she looked with puzzlement and concern. And when she tried to breach the distance between us—and she often did, sending me cards and letters at school, buying me gifts—I sulkily rejected her. For I was no longer a good girl; I was flunking out of college and wildly out of control. She knew it and I knew it and neither of us knew what to do about me. My drinking had accelerated, and I searched for someone to restrain me, some man who might take me in hand and put me back together.

The boys I dated, however, were just like me, party boys, dropouts. The only "real" man I had ever loved had broken my seventeen-year-old heart one Christmas holiday in 1956.

Fourteen

*W*e met in Camden on a frosty December night. I was full of myself, a senior in high school and president of the school and very, very pretty. I wore a bright red chiffon dress, with pearls around my neck.

We were at a Christmas party, and my friend Penny pointed him out. He was a wonderful-looking boy—blond crew cut, soft skin, and aquiline features. His eyes were crinkly and blue and he looked shy and alone standing near a group of young men. There was Joe Williams and Anc Boykin, Bratton DeLoach and Red DuBose—all Camden boys home for the holidays, preening—young peacocks. There was Frankie Wooten, a blond Rock Hudson, who had been my Easter vacation boyfriend last year. Frankie's father had died, and I found that dramatic. Lonely men, men in pain—they moved me like a fly to honey.

"That's Tommy Charlton," said Penny. "He's staying with the Williamses out at Mulberry. He's a friend of Joe's from Yale. He's an orphan."

An orphan! What a boon—a shy and handsome orphan! He drove me home that night, and kissed me. I would have asked him in, but I was afraid my parents might hear, might catch me necking. That is what we did in the fifties—we "necked." The next step was "petting," but that was very tricky for a Catholic girl—it involved the loosening of clothes. And, oh, my, the clothes we wore!

First there was a stiff undergarment called a Merry Widow, all nylon with spines that cupped your breasts and traveled down your midriff. It did, however push up your breasts and make them look fuller. You hooked it on in back. Under this you wore underpants or sometimes a panty girdle. Either the Merry Widow or the panty girdle was equipped with garters, brutal little metal clasps that made marks on your thighs. These attached to nylon stockings, leaving a tasty wedge of white thigh flesh exposed. Nylons seemed always to run, so you never went out without a vial of colorless nail polish in your purse, to stop the ladder from racing down your leg. Stockings also had seams, which you had to straighten constantly. You wore high heels with painful pointed toes, and your ankles wobbled when you walked. Over this armor, we wore tight-cinched strapless dresses. Sometimes they had tulle skirts underneath to make them stick out even farther. It was all very prickly, and very complicated, especially for sweaty wandering hands.

The next night Tom and I met again. It was a coon hunt, an excuse to drink whiskey from flasks, wear blue jeans, ride in Jeeps in the starlight, and pretend that we were looking for raccoon. The idea was that hounds, released into the night, would pick up the scent of a raccoon and give chase. When one was treed, the handlers would hold it captive with flashlights for the kill. Fortunately, the raccoon usually outsmarted the dogs, no blood had to be spilled, and the great chase simply became a wild midnight party, which was, of course, the whole point of the exercise.

The Carolina woods are spectacular at night, cold and dry, full of pine perfuming the air and the cries of the hound dogs racing wild and determined. And there is actually mistletoe growing from the scattered oaks.

You meet out at the Mill Pond, twenty, twenty-four young men and women standing in the dark night with shotguns loaded, safeties on. An enormous bonfire licks and flashes at our faces. We huddle there for warmth. There is a white overseer holding back the hounds, and with the help of two colored men, the dogs, trembling with excitement, are herded onto the back of two trucks. You hang back, the girls with the girls, the boys apart, some of them passing a flask back and forth. Out of the corner of your eye you seek him out—he is there! You knew he would be there. And shyly, he smiles and motions you to the Jeep he's riding in. You keep yourself from running to him; you walk over as if it has just occurred to you that maybe you and he will ride together. You pretend you know what you're doing with the shotgun. He takes it from under your arm and breaks it open and spills the shells into his hand. Oh, his hands . . .

"Never ride in a car with a loaded gun," he says.

"Oh, no," I whisper, "never . . ." My heart is beating so that I can barely hear myself speak. I am breathless in his presence, this strong, handsome man, this older man—a senior at Yale. Why, I am only just finishing high school. I stand on the running board and he reaches with both arms to pull me up beside him. I sit close to him, as close as I can get, too shy to say anything. He is timid also, and we ride silent into the woods.

The boys drive the Jeeps hard, making sharp turns through dark alleys of trees, spinning in the sand. The girls laugh and squeal with pretended fear. You fall against this man you want, the curves are sharp, and, heart thudding, you kiss, and hold each other tight, trying to feel, to feel through the layers of sweaters and windbreakers and scarves and gloves. Tom's nose is cold. I think he has a beautiful nose, like David's, like that of every statue of every beautiful man you see in Italy and Greece.

I looked for Tom at the train station platform. I thought he would come to tell me good-bye, to ask for my address at school, to ask when he might see me again. He didn't come. There were others there, partying, for every afternoon in Camden during the holidays, spontaneous parties occurred at the railroad station as you waited for the Silver Meteor to take you back north. Camden was in many ways a resort—families coming south for vacation, and college and prep school students traveling back and forth from school. A baggage cart would be loaded with liquor, glasses and ice appear from nowhere, and at least a dozen carloads of friends gathered to wish you bon voyage, to say good luck, come back soon, see you, darlin'—see you spring vacation, see you Easter, see you at the Carolina Cup, Camden's great steeplechase, the first of the season.

My friend Penny called me at Noroton from Sarah Lawrence College soon after the Christmas holiday to tell me, gently, that Tom was engaged. To a girl from Vassar called Joan. It wasn't possible; I adored him—and all the while I had simply been Tom's holiday diversion. I was disconsolate. I *wanted* him. What else could I do but pray? I set out to say a novena to the Virgin Mary. Nine prayers nine times a day for nine days? I can't quite remember. You are supposed to smell the scent of roses at the end of the novena if Our Lady has heard your prayers. I didn't smell the roses, but I did get Tom.

Two years later, in Camden in the spring of 1958, my same friend Penny, now engaged to Tom's friend Joe Williams, called me to say, "Guess who's here visiting Joe at Mulberry? And guess who's not engaged anymore?"

My heart flipped. "Oh, no . . . Tommy Charlton?"

"The very same," said Penny, "and we're bringing him out to Cool Springs to the red dog party."

"Oh, gosh . . ."

"And, Carol," said Penny teasing, "he's asked about you."

Six changes of costume later, I drove out to Cool Springs with my date, won thirty dollars at red dog, and accepted Tom's request for a date the following night. Having graduated from the Yale School of Engineering, he was now fulfilling his ROTC requirement in the Marine Corps at Camp Lejeune. He had one more year to go. He seldom returned to Savannah, where he had been brought up and spent most of his holidays with the Williams family in Camden.

Oh, but he was eligible—a fine southern lineage to impress my mother and an Ivy League education to please my brothers and sisters! And handsome, and strong. I sensed also that there was hurt there, and a deep solitude. The loss of his parents had been devastating, his mother dying of leukemia when he was thirteen, his father suffering depression and dying five years later. Tom's sister once told me, "Daddy died with Mother—it just took him some years to get there."

Tom himself didn't discuss this. He didn't speak of personal matters or of painful events. But then, neither did

The receiving line at Tom's and my wedding, April 4, 1959 (Kamschatka, Camden, South Carolina).

I, and neither did anyone I knew. I understood that kind of reticence; it was familiar, even comfortable. I would simply love him with all my heart, ease his pain, and please him. Forever. Tom and I reached that decision after five or six dates, the short, passionate encounters we managed every month or so. For he was in North Carolina and I in Purchase, New York, working as hard as I could at flunking out of Manhattanville.

Tom rescued me from the tatters of my college career. I had found a man I could rely on, a man strong enough to contain my distress, the aching heart I seemed forever to limp around with. We married two years later on a sunny April day in 1959 in Camden, the azalea gardens massed with coral flowers. My mother took off her mourning

clothes, wore a pretty lavender dress and matching hat, my
brothers and sisters came south, festive, affectionate (and
quite possibly relieved that someone else now had me in
charge). My brother John gave me away. In the limousine
to the church, he brought out a flask and we both had a
quick snort. I spoke my marriage vows on waves of Miss
Dior and Chivas Regal. I wore the same lace veil that my
sisters had been married in. It had been given to my father
many years before in Mexico by a Madame Paloma, maid-
in-waiting to the empress Carlotta. I wore a satin gown
with a nineteen-inch waist.

I was beautiful and besotted, Tom was handsome and
strong and proud. And we had barely made each other's
acquaintance. We were young, ill suited, and unable to
talk, still children ourselves, self-absorbed and needy.

Cutting the cake . . .

Fifteen

We spent our honeymoon at Green Turtle Cay in the Bahamas, bone fishing. Hot sun, salt skin, rum at night, and lovemaking. The suitcase with my "trousseau"—flowered frocks, toreador pants, silk nighties—stayed unopened. I wore a bathing suit or nothing at all. I learned to fish, though the sand sharks swimming through the shallows frightened me. But Tom said they would not bother us, and everything Tom said I believed.

In Nassau, on our way home, in a proper hotel, I saw that Blind Blake, the calypso musician, was playing at a nightclub there. Which of my pretty new dresses would I wear? Which shoes? Tom returned to the room, and excitedly I told him about Blind Blake and what fun it would be to hear him. A flash of irritation crossed his face, "What makes you think we're going to see him?" he said. It was final—there was no discussion. I cried, and along the way, I would learn to stop asking, never to ask, never to say what I wanted because the answer was sure to be no. There was a rigidity there that I had mistaken for strength; I suspect also that my own passivity and neediness overwhelmed him—would have overwhelmed anybody.

We returned to New Haven, to the first floor of a dark Victorian house. Tom was working at Yale Admissions, but he was really there to row. He wanted to compete in the Olympics again. Tom had been the captain of the Yale crew that had won the gold medal at the 1956 Olympics. Rowing was his first love, and after that, hunting and fishing. Tom was my first (only) love. I played house, displayed all our wedding gifts about the dark paneled walls of the apartment, which took on a Tiffany & Company country gift shop ambience—everything in place but the price tags. For our first meal I bought frozen fish sticks, frozen french fries, frozen peas, and a frozen apple pie. One oven, three temperature settings. Tom taught me to use the stove; Tom taught me to use the washing machine. Tom, though he had been brought up with servants himself, was astounded at my ignorance about the simplest of household chores. But because we were still in love, he found it amusing, enjoyed teaching me things, acting as my mentor—later, my childishness would pall, my childishness and my financial independence.

Tom was thrifty and I, a spendthrift. And so, instead of asking him for money, coming to him, learning to ask and to negotiate, I simply began to spend my own money when I needed something. Later, in Virginia, when our second child was born, Tom refused to buy a washer and dryer. And so I simply called Sears and ordered and paid for them myself. I thought the lawn looked bare, he didn't—I went to the nursery and ordered five trees. I had no understanding then about issues of control, no sense that I might be threatening his authority and undermining his role as husband and breadwinner. In the 1950s gender roles were still rigidly intact, and most women were given allowances. My financial independence began to open a rift that neither of us recognized or understood. We certainly didn't talk about it—we didn't discuss "personal" things.

Not even at the beginning. Tom worked days and rowed evenings. I sat dully at home learning to use appliances and reading *The Joy of Cooking*—and wondering what to do for the rest of the interminable day. I was twenty years old. I didn't ask my sisters what they did at home all day, I didn't ask my mother. This was, I supposed, marriage and what married women did; no one had said it had to be interesting.

The quiet didn't matter much because very soon I had someone else to commune with, a tiny embryo growing in my body. The wonder of it! I sat on the bus, coming home from the dapper obstetrician, enthralled by my condition. They must know, the people sitting apathetically around me, waiting for their stops—they must sense that inside me a miracle had occurred: I had started a baby. My sister Maureen was the first to know. Then I called my mother, and then the others. Now I had fully joined the family: I was pregnant. I would become pregnant seven times in the next five and a half years. I was a Buckley, wasn't I?

It no longer mattered that I knew no one, that I had nothing to do and nothing to occupy my mind. It didn't matter because every second, every hour, of my pregnancy was wondrous. And far from worrying about my figure, my swelling belly and the mysterious movements and turnings within it filled me with pride of accomplishment. Perhaps it was this I had been waiting for, this that would give me worth and meaning.

The pain is different, not the same as the pre-labor contractions I have been having. It is a penetrating wound

113

deep inside. I am lying in a tiny white room on a very small, hard white cot, the insides of my thighs still sticky from the breaking water.

A young man comes in. He is a stranger, for my own doctor has chosen this week to go skiing in Vermont. He introduces himself as a medical resident. He has a birthmark on his face; he has a doughy face and a bored expression.

"How often are the pains coming?"

"They don't, Doctor—I have a pain that doesn't go away. Inside. It just stays. . . ."

He sighs, lifts up my hospital gown, and takes the flesh of my distended stomach between his thumb and his forefinger. He pinches it: "You're not even in labor—look, it's not hard!"

"But," I say timidly, feeling stupid, knowing that I have failed him, that I am not doing this the way it's meant to be done, and so I continue in a tiny voice, "it still hurts—something hurts."

I look down so as not to see the disdain in his eyes. I concentrate on not crying out, not showing how much it hurts.

A nurse comes in. She puts a cold stethoscope against my belly. The doctor has turned away, irritated, bored. . . .

"Doctor!" she looks up, takes his elbow to turn him around. "The heartbeat is dropping. One-twenty down to sixty!"

The doctor flushes. He calls in a loud voice: "This is an emergency," and to me, "You're going to have to have surgery. You have to sign first. Hurry up, we don't have time to waste!"

I don't understand how it is that I am wasting time. I know only that my baby is in jeopardy. The room is sud-

114

*denly jammed with people. I sign a piece of paper clipped
to a board, they throw me on a gurney, race me down a
hall. Metal doors swing open. Inside, there are people wearing masks—someone pours cold brown antiseptic across
my stomach, and a mask is placed on my face.*

"Breathe in. Count backwards after me."

*I do as I'm told. I am twenty-one years old. I make the
sign of the cross and pray: Please save my baby, please save
my baby. . . . Just as I begin to cloud away, a nurse leans
down and whispers: "I am praying, too."*

He was a cunning little boy, a little mouse baby, all
nose and sloping forehead. The traumatic birth was forgotten. Allie drove down from Hartford with a pillowcase
full of novels and a case of Coca-Cola. "They never give
you enough to drink at the hospital," she said. "And you'll
be bored until they let you go home. So, read." Allie was
serving again as my alter-mother. My own mother had
flown up to New York from Camden two days earlier to be
with Maureen—Maureen had given birth to her second
child quite unexpectedly in the bathroom of her New York
apartment.

I didn't read that many of Allie's books, didn't drink
the Coke. I simply stared at little Tommy enraptured,
rubbed his downy cheek with my forefinger, kissed his
wrinkled forehead, adored him.

Maureen's second baby, another little girl, had been
born with my sister Priscilla and Maureen's husband,
Gerry, as most surprised midwives. Waiting for the ambulance to arrive, the pediatrician giving instructions over the
telephone, Gerry and Pitts managed to cut baby Priscilla's
cord after tying it off with a piece of gold Lord & Taylor
Christmas twine—the only string they could find in the

entire apartment. Later, the policeman, riding with Maureen in the ambulance to New York Hospital, said to Gerry, "You got one brave broad for a wife."

Gerry loved telling this story. He loved Maureen. Sometimes we met in Sharon for weekends when Mother moved up from Camden for the summer. How I looked forward to going home and to seeing my brothers and sisters! In a sense, they were still my whole world, a world I now belonged to, for surely I had joined *los grandes* by having a baby of my own. Tom, I suspect, found the weekends boring. He was a doer, a hunter and a fisherman, not a conversationalist, and conversation was what my family did best.

The months passed in a contented haze. Tom and Tommy were the center of my life, and my sister Maureen, my best friend. We spoke almost daily, she from her New York apartment, I from New Haven. She helped me, advised me about baby things, laughed with me, and sympathized when I felt anxious that I was not being the mother I thought I ought to be—which was most of the time. What did I know about being a mother? How would I have known?

With the babies coming now, my sister and I didn't see each other as much as we had. Maureen was immediately pregnant with a third child and I, pregnant with a child I would miscarry. Six weeks after the miscarriage, I was pregnant again with my second son, Buckley. Not seeing Maureen didn't really matter, though, because we had all the time in the world and because, somehow, she was always present with me even when she wasn't there: a guardian angel in the person of a wonderfully happy, ridiculously funny young wife and mother.

Tom told me one evening that he had bought a house

in Charlotte County, Virginia. His family had spent their summers there, and I think his happiest memories were of those carefree days when his parents were alive. His mother's father, Abram Read, was directly descended from Isaac Read, the founder of the county. Isaac, killed in the Revolutionary War, had built a beautiful frame house called Greenfield. The family home was owned jointly by Tom and his brother and sister. For that reason he had chosen to purchase a second home, a brick manse called Do Well.

He would work as a land surveyor in Chase City and farm the land. Tom had an income of his own and so money, making a living, was not a priority. What was, was to return to where he had once had happiness. Tom's dead family had as great a hold on him as my live one had on me, and I deferred to that. He told me that we were moving south, and in June of 1960 we left New Haven for Saxe, Virginia.

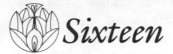# Sixteen

I *sit upstairs in the newly painted nursery in the renovated house that Tom has purchased for us. I am twenty-two and about to deliver my second child. My baby, Tommy, stands in his crib, and I sit on the floor next to him, feeding him the green grapes that Tom's sister has left in the kitchen for us: green grapes, meat loaf smothered in ketchup, and a bottle of dry sherry. Anne and her husband, Stanley, often weekend at Greenfield.*

I am drinking the sherry in a crystal goblet. The house is absolutely still, and it feels cold, here in the middle of nowhere, where there are no lights, no sounds, and the windows are black with night. Tom is not here—it seems to me that he is never here, always out doing something, working in the fields, hunting, fishing.

I look at my adored child. He is a solemn little boy born to silent parents. Tom speaks only when he has something to say; I speak, but it is becoming clearer and clearer that I have nothing very interesting to say and so often it feels as though I'm talking to myself. Tommy's eyes are great blue globes; they look at me, asking? I feel Buckley

*kicking to get out, kicking my belly as hard as he can—he
is a live wire, my little Buckley. I drink more sherry and
begin to sing some silly songs to Tommy: "There's a Lizard
on the Rail," "Pat O'Shea," "I've Been Working on the
Railroad." I don't have much of a voice, but Tommy seems
to think it's just fine and I hope I have covered up the
feelings inside, the desperate, desperate aloneness. For I am
as alone as I have ever been, as alone as I was as a child at
home. The alone man that I have married cannot repair
that. I have simply returned to where I began.*

*The old house creaks. It is wonderfully restored and
finely furnished.*

Do Well, a handsome Georgian house, was built by a
Mr. Gaines in the early nineteenth century. His brother
built Do Better across the swamp. Do Better is gray with
age and disrepair; squatters live there. We have moved here
because of Tom's family, but there is no family, only his
sister once in a while and his brother, Read, when he is on
leave from the Marine Corps. Why are we here? Nowhere.
Four hundred fifty acres of nowhere and a tall brick house
where I am to live forever.

We never discussed it, talked about buying the house
and living there, though I remember visiting it after Tommy
was born, a great brick house standing off the road in a flat
overgrown field—broken pediments, cracked bricks, and
birds nesting inside. It looked like a house that no one had
lived in for years and years and years. The old caretaker,
Mr. Langford, told me later that it had last been inhabited
by "furriners" who worshiped some strange religion with
"an old man in black." They were Hungarian refugees and
the strange religion was my own.

Do Well seemed enormous to me, such a big high-ceilinged house for me and Tommy and the new baby. It overwhelmed me, for I had learned that I could do nothing right. I didn't know how to cook; I took things out of the dryer and they had either shrunk to midget size, or they were stained with another garment's color. I couldn't even have babies properly. Tommy had been born in crisis and only saved by an emergency cesarean. I had miscarried my second child, alone in the Savannah guest house of one of Tom's cousins. The doctor who was called gave me paregoric for pain, which Tom's cousin Aisie supplemented with a couple of martinis. I remember the powerful cramps and finally passing the tiny nucleus of a baby, a little shell-shaped piece of flesh. I didn't cry.

Buckley was born by cesarean section in October of 1961 in a tiny hospital in Farmville, Virginia. I was twenty-two and lost, like a blind person, and that is how I went through those years at Do Well, coming alive only when I had a new baby in my womb or in my arms.

 *Seventeen*

My family came to visit, about one member each year—Charlotte County is not on the way to any-where. Ann and Jim stopped by on their way from Sharon to Camden to visit Mother, and Priscilla, our basset hound, bit their son Billy. Brent and Trish visited without even one of their nine redheaded children, and we had a ball dis-cussing politics and religion and drinking bourbon late into the evening. Brent had just founded the conservative Cath-olic magazine, *Triumph*. Bill had a debate in Richmond and spent the night with us. He shot a snake, I discovered, close to where the children were playing. Tom, who shot most moving things, did not approve of killing the snake. It wasn't the copperhead I had thought it was. It was a "friendly" snake, a friendly copper-headed snake. That af-ternoon, preparing to drive to Richmond for the debate, Bill asked me to come up to his room. "Are these the shoes that go with this suit, Carolita? I forget which ones Patsie told me to wear."

I saw the other members of my family either at Christ-mas in Camden or during the two weeks I spent visiting

Great Elm in summer. There Maureen and I met every year, with armfuls of babies and lots to say. She was still my best friend and confidante. While my mother and I had grown somewhat closer now that I had children of my own, I still wanted to impress her, to let her know that I was successful and doing all the things that she would have wanted me to—that I was a *good* wife and mother.

Soon after Buckley's birth in October 1961, I became pregnant again. I had another miscarriage. I remember feeling depressed and listless. My obstetrician, Dr. Finch, suggested I take an antidepressant. I looked at him with surprise and answered, "No, I'm just fine—tired, that's all."

My daughter Anne was born in October of 1963. I had three children now: Tommy, who was still a quiet boy, anxious, anxious to do the right thing; Buckley, named after my father, who was everywhere, into everything, spirited and rebellious; Anne, a doll-baby baby, delicate, playful, and affectionate. I haven't forgotten the soft, gentle days there, the early greens of spring, and sitting on the porch watching the children tumble out onto the lawn, carefree and full of glee.

But for all that I loved my children, there was a terrible monotony to my days. Tom worked long hours in Chase City, and when he came home, after a hurried supper, he either worked outdoors on the farm or drove out to Greenfield to attend to chores there. I lived in many ways from trip to trip; I lived to leave my home.

Tom and I visited Camden every year for Christmas (duck shooting, quail shooting); I enjoyed seeing my sister Priscilla there, and my mother. The others had too many children to travel now and spent the holidays at home. I took the children to Sharon for a week or two in the sum-

My children at play: Buckley, Anne, Carol, and Tommy (Great Elm, October 1966).

mer, joining Maureen there (no shooting). Tom and I vacationed at Green Turtle Cay (bone fishing) and a couple of times at Ocracoke on the outer banks of North Carolina coast (bass fishing). The island was full of mosquitoes and briny water—I washed the children's diapers by hand. Once we visited Scotland (grouse shooting) and our old friends Joe and Penny Williams in Iran (wild boar shooting). It never occurred to me to explain to Tom that I might prefer vacations that did not entail shooting and fishing; it

123

never even occurred to me that I didn't *like* shooting and fishing. I had few opinions in those days, few likes and dislikes. I maintained an external set of beliefs, religious and political tenets, but inside I had very little that was my own. It was important only to be the person Tom wanted me to be, and to smile.

I kept house. I dressed the children from the Best & Company catalog. Matching corduroy overalls for the boys, embroidered dresses for Anne. It didn't matter, really; there was no one to see them but Rita and me. Rita came in every day, some days she was late and her face was bruised or she limped or moved slowly, deliberately. We did not speak about this. We spoke instead about the children. We both loved my children. I think we were each other's only friend, but as I was white and she was black, we didn't address that.

There were nice people there in the county, but they were older, children grown, and involved in church and civic activities. Most of them were distant relatives of Tom's and they had lived there for generations. Charlotte County was their world—the Presbyterian church, local Democratic politics, their forebears, and the historical association. I was a fish out of water. My good friends the writer Bill Hoffman and his wife, Sue, would move there in 1964. They too were outsiders—they actually read *The New Yorker*. But by then I was becoming sick, my spirit wasted, my self smothered in defeat.

I took the children miles away every Sunday to a mission church. There were no Catholics in the county but me, and the local ministers had preached sermons about the dangers of electing John F. Kennedy president—he would receive his orders, they said, directly from the pope in Rome. It was a sparsely populated rural area whose mores

I didn't understand. Everyone drank, but not when the minister came to call; everyone attended church on Sunday but no one was overly concerned about the plight of the "nigras."

From my earliest days I had wondered about a religion that excluded blacks and Jews. I remember asking my mother as a little girl why Ella and Sally didn't come to church with us. "Because they wouldn't feel comfortable, darling. They feel better in their own churches." And indeed, the Negroes I had known in Camden, all house servants, had seemed content. They were unfailingly courteous and civil, and it never occurred to me that they might be unhappy or deprived. There was a black movie theater, to which we could go if we wanted, and a white one, which they couldn't attend, no matter what. There were black burial grounds and white ones, black and white toilets, black and white hospital wings. No one seemed to mind; no one even seemed to notice.

Charlotte County gave me my first exposure to poor blacks, seeing whole families crowded into shanties, uneducated, and probably cold in winter and hungry, too. This rural poverty was not limited to blacks. Poor whites endured the same conditions, as uneducated and as desolate as the Negroes, with only their white skin to wear as a badge of superiority. Their babies often suffered from "milk anemia" as a result of being nursed well into their third or fourth year. They were fat, listless, and apathetic, their skin an eerie blue-white from lack of protein.

I looked. More often, I looked away, too timid to question or speak my mind, for I was cowardly still and wanted to belong. I assuaged my conscience by paying Rita twice the wages other maids received (and swearing her to secrecy). We Catholics, tiny handful that we were, had a

125

fairly liberal priest, and because of him there were two or three black families who also attended Mass at the mission. That made me feel better. The integration battle on the television news seemed a thousand miles away from Charlotte County, like everything else that was happening in the world. My own paltry contribution to the cause was to draw the line at racist jokes.

This racial bias among our acquaintances was quite simply what came with being southern. In other ways they were good and charitable people, the men running small businesses (*very* small businesses) and the women keeping house. The biscuits and pies were baked to perfection, the gardens, tended and bountiful. Once a year one of the old homes was opened to visitors by the Association for the Preservation of Virginia Antiquities; once a month you might visit the movie house thirty-five miles away in Prince Edward County. The only pediatrician lived seventy miles away in Lynchburg. There was one restaurant, at Sheldon's Motel in Keysville. I did my grocery shopping in Drakes Branch—it had a grocery store, a liquor store, a Ford dealership, and the *Charlotte Gazette,* a weekly paper with mostly local news and social announcements. I remember the notice that a little Tommy Jay had returned from the hospital "where he suffered a complication of troubles."

One November afternoon as I was driving into Drakes Branch to buy groceries, the children tucked in the back seat, an announcer's voice cut through the music to announce President Kennedy's assassination—"assassination attempt." I raced home and sat with the children in my bedroom watching the terrible events unfold. I telephoned Maureen. The next morning I packed up the children and drove the thirty-five miles to our mission church in Keysville, and there a handful of us Catholics prayed for his

126

soul, beseeched the angels to guide him to the joys of everlasting life. Many of us embraced, many stayed on to say the rosary. I shared with these strangers more than I could ever share with my husband or with our Protestant friends.

Once in a while one of Tom's friends visited from as far away as Washington. These men had all rowed at Yale, either with Tom in the Olympics or during our year in New Haven. Tom maintained strong friendships with his male friends. He was comfortable with men, what people used to call "a man's man." Tom's friends brought me legs of lamb—a rarity in Virginia—and their wives and girlfriends and I gossiped and laughed. At night, after the children were asleep, we drank, argued politics, talked books—little glimmers of the life I had once been accustomed to. Tom and I did fine with other people around; alone, we were becoming more and more silent—he, absorbed with his job and the outdoor maintenance of Do Well; I, with the babies.

I did know two Republicans, working-class men, and together we set up a Goldwater headquarters in Keysville in the spring of 1964. I was elected to run it, meaning that I was elected to sit there day after day. Nobody ever came in, and so I had a lot of Goldwater bracelets, elephant pins with black horn-rim glasses, and bumper stickers collecting dust. If our acquaintances found my solitary devotion amusing, they didn't say. They wouldn't—for that is the way of southerners, never to offend openly while smiling behind their hands.

My family, on the other hand, was very involved in the Goldwater campaign; no one had come along since Robert Taft to engender such approval. Maureen and I spoke weekly by phone—we wished we could be more involved in the campaign, but she had just had her fifth baby, Billy, and I was pregnant again, three months after my daughter Anne's birth. Maureen and I talked babies and Goldwater. We planned our summer Sharon visit together. She and Gerry and their five children had now moved to Scarsdale. The thought of being with her at Great Elm in the summer, having her there, kept me going; Maureen was my lifeline, her presence even at the end of a telephone line sustained me. She kept me laughing, she kept me in balance.

It started insidiously, in the winter of 1964. Tom was away for the night at a surveyors' meeting in Richmond. It was a cold March night, and I had just put the three children to bed. I took a glass of sherry to my bedroom—it had begun, my drinking alone at night. I was reading—some novel, I suppose, perhaps a mystery. I was aware, suddenly, that I hadn't felt the baby move. For how long? How long? I held my breath because this was surely my imagination. I was bone-tired; maybe the baby was too? There was nothing, no movement, my womb was deathly still.

Tyree Finch, Dr. Finch, had become my best and closest friend. Whom else did I see with such regularity? He delivered Buckley and Anne by cesarean and treated me during my second miscarriage. Tyree brought me champagne to drink and Chesterfields to smoke, right in the hospital. His office had a leather hassock. The top opened up. Tommy and Buckley fought to be the first to climb inside, wrestling each other to the floor, and in the fun of it, forgetting the hassock altogether. Anne was in my arms. I took her with me into the examination room.

"The baby has died. We never know why this happens. We'll try to induce you, Carol, but if you haven't started labor by now, you probably won't until term."

Three more months to carry this dead child.

"Often," he continued, taking my hand in his, "this is

a very depressing experience for a woman. It can lead to depression. Call me anytime. Call me anytime, Carol, you hear?"

He could have been talking to a zombie, a smiling zombie with dimples and pretty blue eyes. What is depressing? I'm fine—I was always "just fine" in those days, bright and brittle, busy, busy, busy doing nothing, too busy to eat. I endured my first full labor three months later to produce a dead little boy.

Three weeks after that, Maureen died.

 *Eighteen*

*H*er maid, Georgia Cobb, let herself into Maureen's kitchen in Scarsdale one July morning in 1964. There she found Billy still in his high chair; Ann and little Gerry, two and three, milling about the kitchen; and Patricia and Priscilla, ages five and four, trying to make an ice bag. Maureen lay on the floor in a coma. She had complained of a headache, and the little girls had tackled the freezer to find some ice to put on her head.

We were together again, my family, sitting vigil once more in a hospital waiting room. With the exception of Thanksgivings at Great Elm, a holiday I spent in Virginia, we seldom came together anymore; the family had simply grown too big. Aloise brought games to play, Scrabble, a jigsaw puzzle. Allie never arrived anywhere without a sack of something to do. We sat, we walked the corridors, attempting talk, turning our eyes away from Gerry's stricken face. On June 28, Maureen and Gerry had celebrated their sixth wedding anniversary. Maureen was thirty-one years old.

I wrote to one of the Sacred Heart nuns, Mother

Miller, to ask for her prayers. Shortly after I closed the envelope, the neurologist called us together.

"Are you going to operate?" asked my mother. She knew that one operated on brain hemorrhages. They had operated on my father that last time at Lenox Hill Hospital.

The young man looked at her and said bluntly, "There is nothing to operate on. Her brain is destroyed—it's gone. There is nothing to do but wait."

And pray.

That night my mother and I shared a bedroom. I don't know where the others went to. Did they stay in hotels or drive back to their homes in New York and Connecticut? I know that that evening it was only Mother and me. She asked me to kneel with her and say the rosary for Maureen's return to health. I looked at her. Three weeks before, I had given birth to a stillborn baby boy in Farmville, Virginia, and my faith was such that I asked the local priest to baptize his remains. I believed he was in heaven, I believed that I had a son in heaven with the other two children I had miscarried. But Maureen! My beloved Maureen with the dead brain.

Joining my mother at the bedside, kneeling beside her, I complied and spoke the words with an empty heart: "Holy Mary, Mother of God, pray for us sinners now and at the hour of our death."

What were we praying for? To whom were we praying? Nothing would bring Maureen back, my laughing, loving sister. It was finished. I continued for a few years to practice my religion by rote. And then, quite simply, I stopped. It was not a dramatic decision, not a thought-out one; one Sunday, I missed Mass. A couple of Sundays later, I missed it again. By 1970, I stopped pretending altogether.

I cry once, at the funeral. I return to Do Well dry-eyed. Tom tries to care for me. I will not cry again for Maureen for many years, I do not speak of her, don't mention her name. I am "just fine." Only the strangest thing is happening to my body: it is beginning to freeze. I call it bursitis (I blame it on the damp, chilly little Goldwater office in Keysville). Soon, I can no longer raise my arms. Tom has to help me get dressed. In the morning, walking down the back stairs to the kitchen, I take the steps one at a time. My hips are frozen, too, and the upper joints of my legs pop in and out. My condition worsens, bizarre and frightening. I make an appointment to see Tyree. He calls in a specialist from Richmond; I have rheumatoid arthritis, the crippling form.

It wasn't arthritis, though. My skeleton had become "fixed, flinty, formal, frightful, frigid, frozen, granitic, grave, hard, harsh, icy, immalleable": all the symptoms of rigor mortis. I believe now that that is what I suffered and how I sought to join my dead sister. Unable to grieve for Maureen and unable to accept her death, I had no other means to stay with her except by letting a part of me die too.

I woke up a few months later, symptom-free. I was twenty-five, I had started my baby Carol, and the cortisone coursing through my newly pregnant body had eradicated the symptoms, the cortisone and the gift of a new life. My little Carol was a Hummel baby, serious of mien like the little faces on the figurines, an observer, deliberate and gentle. I loved her intensely, for I knew she was to be my last—the many pregnancies and four surgeries had necessitated a hysterectomy. I don't think Tyree trusted me not to get pregnant again.

The following June, John's wife, Ann, ran down to the lake below their house and fell dead of a heart attack. She was thirty-eight years old and left three children and a husband who would never recover from his loss. My family congregated at the Salisbury cemetery for the burial. I had a minute to join Allie before she left for Hartford. I had asked her to be my daughter Carol's godmother. I had brought a picture. Allie looked at me with tired eyes and said, "But of course—she's sweet, Carol. Is she as sweet as she looks?"

The following January, Aloise suffered a massive brain hemorrhage. She complained of an excruciating headache. Ben and her son Jim drove her to the hospital emergency room in Hartford. Allie's brain hemorrhage took two weeks to kill her. I stayed at her house and remember night after night playing Monopoly and Scrabble with her older children—Allie would have liked that.

My mother and my brothers and sisters stayed together at a hotel, and we met each day, taking turns at hospital duty. There was a sense of shock, a numbness that we were once again together, awaiting death. We were extremely quiet, crowded into the small waiting room. There were no games to play, no jigsaw puzzles to tackle, nothing to take our minds off our comatose sister in Intensive Care. There was no Allie to supply us with puzzles and games, no Allie to nudge the hospital staff, no Allie to make us laugh.

My mother was heartbroken. Aloise, her firstborn and mainstay. Aloise and Mother had begun traveling together every summer. Sometimes my aunt Inez joined them, or Priscilla or Jane or Tish, but it was Allie who had gotten Mother up on a camel in Egypt, Allie who had hidden in a crypt in the Parthenon and lost her way out, Allie who gave rude Parisians what for. Allie—the bane of all hypocrites! When she died, a lot of our laughter went with her.

133

The funeral Mass and burial were held in Sharon, Allie put to rest next to our sister Maureen. I remember nothing of that entire day, from morning to night. It remains an empty space. It was too much for me to bear, this second, ritual reenactment of Maureen's death. And so my mind closed down, amnesiac.

Nineteen

Mornings in Virginia I wake to the sound of my baby Carol crying in her crib. She is hungry, wanting her bottle. Anne, in the crib next to her, is making morning singsong, coos, and little cries, pulling at the music box, dropping her dolls and stuffed animals one by one to the floor. "Toy, Mommy, toy," she says, wanting me to pick them up and start the game all over again. My head is thick with sleep. I want a cigarette, I want nothing but to go back to bed.

Upstairs on the third floor I hear a howl of outrage. Tommy has taken Buckley's toy, Buckley has taken Tommy's toy—I hear bare feet racing across the ceiling, screeching, yelling, a crash, a scream. The first fight of the day. I put Carol to my shoulder and hitch Anne against my hip; I can feel that her pajamas are wet—both babies need changing. I move to the stairs and call up, "Stop it! Stop it, now, boys! It's time for breakfast. Come downstairs for breakfast. . . ."

I change the girls. They want to play, they kick and gurgle. I don't feel like playing—I never play anymore with

135

the children. I just get done what I have to do. Even that feels like too much. I lift Carol up by the ankles, put the folded diaper between her chubby legs, pin the corners, reach for the rubber pants. Anne runs away with them, teasing, jealous that I am changing Carol first. I hold Carol on the changing table and grab Anne's leg, pulling her back to reach for the rubber pants. She falls, she cries heart-wrenching tears, hurt, betrayed. I am her mommy; I have knocked her down. Oh, God . . .

I scream at the boys to stop it! I scream at them to come down for breakfast. I place Carol on the floor where she cannot fall, and take Anne into my arms. The only thing is, she is not crying anymore. I am. Tears come down my face, for I am mean and bad, cruel to my children, angry. I cannot stand it anymore, being so mean and bad; I cannot stand the feeling I carry—somewhere just at the center of my navel there is an empty black ache, a sensation worse than pain that I carry every waking moment. Failure dogs my steps, and inadequacy. Had I been enough, wouldn't my mother have loved me? I am what I have always suspected, a nothing, a nobody. I have a husband I cannot love and children to whom I cannot show my love. There is nothing left in me to love—it has all been taken away and buried in the ground.

I hug Anne against my stomach, against my jagged cesarean scar. She struggles to move away; I am holding her too hard. The boys, downstairs at last, peer into the doorway, angry little faces, pouting, needing what I cannot give them anymore. Nothing relieves the emptiness, not the coffee, not cigarettes, not the booze I drink every night. I have no one to call, no one to share this panic with, no friend. For I am filled with shame at the failure of my being, and no one must know.

136

In the afternoons when the children are napping, the groceries bought, Rita helping with the laundry, I experience a restless claustrophobia. Rita has begun looking at me in a funny way, pity in her eyes. She touches me more; sometimes she hugs me. I walk out to the porch where the Sears Roebuck cane chairs are. I arrange and rearrange them. Back and forth, sofa here, armchair there, armchair with matching ottoman to the other side; no, not right. I start again, sofa on this side, chair there, chair and ottoman here. But no, that's not right. I start again. One square porch, one sofa, one chair with ottoman, one chair without ottoman. How many combinations, then? I start again. Sometimes it will take two hours, rearranging the porch furniture, sometimes it will take until the children wake, wanting the mother who is no longer there.

When Tom comes home at night from work, it will be even worse. We have supper mostly in silence. After supper he goes out again, either to mow the fields on his bush-hog or down to his office to tie fishing flies or to clean his guns . . . or to get away from me. I can't blame him. I have become numb by now, aching for sleep, the only thing that takes my pain away. I sleep as far away from him as I can. My back turned, my back rigid to ensure that I won't be touched. One of these nights—time runs together, it races and it stays the same, a lodestone of days—I pick up the phone and call Tyree at home. "I think I need a doctor," I say, "a psychiatrist."

It was a painful admission. I didn't know people who went to psychiatrists, "had therapy," went to counselors—weak, self-indulgent, crazy people. Like me? For I was now one of them, and though I knew I wasn't delusional—didn't see things that weren't there or hear voices in empty rooms—I supposed I had a suppressed kind of craziness: a suffocating, inchoate madness, stuffed deep inside and just waiting to pounce. I knew I had to be very vigilant to keep the madness down and keep it from shattering me.

Dr. Foster, the Richmond psychiatrist to whom Tyree had referred me, was kindly and concerned. I remember being so anxious that I could barely speak, barely answer his questions, and when he asked me why I had made the appointment, I mumbled something about my marriage, about my marriage and what a bad mother I was. I left the office with prescriptions for Librium, Elavil, and a sleeping medication. I took them as ordered though sleep was not my problem—it was my waking hours that threw me for a loop.

It was the spring of 1967. Carol was almost two years old; Anne, three and a half; Buckley, five and a half; and Tommy, just seven. I wasn't planning my trip to Sharon that summer; I wasn't planning anything. Though I spoke more often on the phone to my sisters Jane and Patricia, and to Priscilla, I had nothing really to tell them. My truth was too painful to reveal, and as I had no understanding of how this state had evolved, I couldn't find the words to speak of it. "I am bad and I hate myself." What kind of a thing was that to say to people who loved you? When I spoke to Mother, I continued to pretend that everything was fine. For my mother was sad and we all felt protective of her, as parents are meant to feel about their children.

And Tom. What had I to say to him? "I'm sorry, I'm sorry, I'm sorry . . ."

A week after I saw Dr. Foster, my friend Sue Hoffman called to tell me that an acquaintance of ours, Sarah, had attempted suicide. I was stunned. Ever-smiling Sarah, with her lovely husband and fine children! Why, she had looked perfectly happy, not a worry in the world. I became obsessed by this event, obsessed and also fascinated. I talked and talked about it to Tom that night, though it was hardly the kind of subject that interested him. He went up to bed before me.

I stayed in the library, drinking. A panic had begun to build, a strange excitement that frightened and exhilarated me. I went to the telephone and called Dr. Foster. I told his answering service that I must reach him. It was unlike me to make that kind of demand, but my agitation was such that I knew I needed help. He called back within the hour.

"Someone I know," I said, "a friend of mine tried to kill herself."

"And you? How are you, Mrs. Charlton? How are you feeling?" he asked.

"I'm scared," I said. "I don't know why, but I am very, very scared."

He asked me to put Tom on the phone.

It is pouring rain, hard to see through the windshield, and we are traveling an unknown route, through Richmond, to the grounds of Westbrook Hospital. I am hugging myself, curled into a ball against the far door. I am numb—I feel nothing but cold. Tom's neck and shoulders are rigid as he maneuvers the car adroitly around the water pooled on the highway, rivers of water that spray to the right and left. The car is cold. Tom and I have different thermostats.

I can't remember if there are gates. It is the middle of the night. The next two times I return, it will be by ambulance; the last time I am unconscious. Of course, there must be gates! This is an insane asylum, a psychiatric hospital for crazy people. I don't feel crazy—I feel exhausted to death. Too soon we stop at a white cottage, and except

139

for the giant locks on the doors, it looks like any person's cozy house. There is a nice little porch on the front, and a nice little nurse unlocks the front door. There is a light on in the parlor, just one—the rooms above are silent, their occupants sedated and waiting.

A young physician, not Dr. Foster, interviews me. The nurse has taken Tom into another room. Why am I here?

Why am I here? I don't know.

I don't know. I don't know. . . .

He takes my blood pressure. He listens to my heart. I am given an injection and walked upstairs. The nurse leads me into a bedroom and tells me to unpack tomorrow. I ask her if I can call my children. I haven't said good-bye—they won't know why I am gone!

"Goodness," she says, "at twelve-thirty at night?"

The body in the bed next to mine stirs. Silently I put on my nightie and climb between the cool sheets. Why am I here? The sedative has begun to work, and my limbs are heavy with it. I begin to float into nothingness. That is where I want to be, that is what I crave.

I start awake when the bedside light is snapped on. A young woman in a pajama top and nothing else is standing by my bed, staring at me. I am frightened, but my voice and tongue won't work; the drug has semiparalyzed me.

"I'm leaving tomorrow," she says, expressionless. "I'm a paranoid schizophrenic."

Twenty

*I*t doesn't take long to get used to a hospital routine, to regress and do what you're told and feel safe again like a child. Get up, get dressed, take pills, have breakfast, wait in the room for your doctor, wait in the room for your doctor, wait in the room for your doctor. . . . Go to lunch, take your pills, go to occupational therapy, "rest," take your pills, go to supper, hang out in the parlor, take your pills, sleep—like the dead people you have become.

I still didn't know why I was there, and I certainly didn't know what to tell the doctors. What I did not tell them, nor did they ask, was that I had become a heavy drinker who, if not physically dependent, was by now emotionally dependent on the soothing—and depressant—properties of alcohol. In fact, never once during my year and a half of psychiatric hospitalizations was I questioned about my alcohol intake or about my need for it. I told my doctor, instead, about the time I was molested as a child. I don't know why I told him except that that was what I thought psychiatrists were after.

I remembered the incident clearly, could recall the fear and pain and the "dirty" feelings I felt during and after. There was no repression of this memory. I knew the man; I had known him for most of my life. Who he was I would never tell. It happened only once, and I knew even then, young as I was, that it would not happen again, or most probably wouldn't. It was a onetime occurrence born of too much drink and too deeply repressed sexuality.

Drs. Foster and Gayle didn't seem very interested in that. They didn't express interest in much of what I said. Often they seemed to observe me in virtual silence. They were, I now understand, analytically trained, following the neutral tradition of Freudians, attempting never to intrude on a patient's projections and transference. But while analysis is an engrossing and liberating experience, it is not helpful for crisis intervention. I didn't need silence—I lived in silence. What I needed were explanations, answers. When I told them that my husband was a good man and that the trouble was with me, they, in their silence, seemed to agree. When I told them that my children were wonderful but I was a bad mother, they seemed to agree. When I told them that my brothers and sisters were all born brilliant and knew more about everything than I did, they listened. . . . When I told them that anyway I was fat (ninety-eight pounds dressed), they nodded.

One morning I had a letter from Tyree Finch. A loving note, apologizing for not visiting, stating that it had been a "killer of a week at the office." He ended, "You are a very special person, Mrs. Charlton, With love always, Tyree." It was Dr. Gayle's morning. I wasn't as fond of him as I was of Dr. Foster, though Dr. Gayle was young and very, very handsome. His other patients adored him. This is, in shrink-language, called a "transference"; in patient language this means getting the hots for your doctor.

I told Dr. Gayle about the letter. For a fleeting second I imagined that his face paled. He asked to see it. He read it very slowly. When he handed it back, we continued my "therapy," my telling him about my failings, and his nodding sagely. Our sessions never lasted long, Dr. Gayle's and mine. I strolled downstairs and onto the porch. It was a sunny May morning and I realize now that the Arab-Israeli War had begun, but nothing much penetrates you in a mental hospital. I was encased in self-absorption and psychotropic medicine. There was a *Richmond News-Leader* on the porch swing. I picked it up just to scan the headlines. That is about all you can do when you are in depression; you cannot concentrate. Everything is muted and wrapped in fog except for the raw pain you hurry to bury and bury, deeper, deeper. . . . Hide it. Whatever you do, don't ever expose it. Otherwise you will lose control and your self will explode into tiny fragments and blow away like dust.

On the front page I saw the headline, middle of the page on the left-hand side: "Prince Edward Obstetrician, Tyree Finch, a Suicide."

They lie. Doctors lie. They do not tell you the truth. They are like parents and nurses and brothers and sisters—they don't tell you the truth. Even Tyree lied to me in his letter: "I want to see you soon," he wrote. I have been excluded by lies, lies and abandonment. And death, the final abandonment, stalks the people I love and the people I need and count on. For me, to care is to lose. This is true because I am bad; I am excluded and left behind because I am bad; it is my badness that makes people die. And so my depression whispered, nasty, hateful, distorting and twisting. . . .

143

He had wrapped his head in bandages so as not to make a mess and had shot himself through the mouth. He had left some letters; mine was among them. I told Miss Love, the head nurse, that I had a headache and wouldn't be going to lunch. I went upstairs to my room, smashed a cut-glass vase, and slashed my wrists. Not very skillfully . . .

At least now we knew why I was there. Because I was a very bad person who deserved to die. There were other "bad" women like me at Oak Cottage as well—Nancy, intense and funny, our group clown; Meredith, a wistful young woman of my age who had married an older man. I supposed Meredith's husband was in his sixties—I couldn't imagine our willowy Meredith in his old man's arms. There was a tall young woman whose name I can't remember. She was another "everything's just fine" kind of person, extremely neat and personable, a real Virginia lady. It was only when I saw her in her bathing suit that I realized she must be very sick and dying. Perhaps she had come here to die—how sad!

I had never seen an anorexic before, rib cage exposed, great knobs of kneebones because there is no flesh to cover them, only concave thighs and calves with eroded muscle, like a person with paralysis. The body devours its own muscle to survive, and what had been her buttocks now hung loose and flaccid, empty sacks of skin. She was thirty years old, and she too had a loving family and a perfect life. Only she didn't think she was bad, like me, or like Meredith—she thought she was fat.

In occupational therapy we mingled with the other patients. I made Indian moccasins for the children and octopuses out of braided wool. I carried my children in the recesses of my heart, fearful of seeing them, overwhelmed and filled with guilt at my abandonment of them. And so

I sent cards, I made toys. A young patient called John helped me with the octopuses, and he fell in love with me. That he was homosexual didn't deter him from passing me love notes and sending flowers. I was flattered.

Another young man followed me around; he was on serious medication, the zombie stuff, and he shuffled his feet and stammered when he spoke. They said he had an IQ of 160. They said he was going to stay there a long time. He was from one of the locked wards. I felt sorry for him and tried not to avoid him like the other women. He would come so close when he spoke that I could actually feel his hot breath. He had no boundaries, no sense of personal space. I was told not to become close with him, not to "encourage" him. He had tried to murder his parents.

They sent me home; two weeks later I was back. This time they decided I might have an asymptomatic form of epilepsy, that my self-destructive "attacks" might arise from a brain irregularity. I had neurologic testing; my scalp stayed sticky from it for a solid week. They upped my medication: Elavil, Valium, hypnotics for sleep. They never asked about my drinking, so the next time they sent me home, I did that too. Sometimes Meredith and Nancy and I walked over to the mall adjoining Westbrook Hospital and had cocktails before dinner, so drinking at home couldn't matter much, could it? I began skipping my medication, secreting the pills instead. One here, two there. I hid them. If you had asked me why, I would have looked you straight in the face and told you that I didn't know. I didn't—on a conscious level I had no thoughts of suicide. I knew only that I was sick and bad and that my husband and children deserved something better. My brothers and sisters, too.

They wrote me loving letters; they prayed for me. Jane

and Tish came down to visit and tried to cheer me up and to understand what was happening to me. They urged me to pray and to put my faith in God. But that made me feel worse, talking about God and prayer. I had tried going to confession in a church in Richmond. Tremulously I had mentioned my attempted suicide—the priest told me I would burn in hell forever. "Damned," he said. "Do you comprehend the meaning of damnation?"

I understood hell and damnation but its prospect didn't frighten me as much as the continuance of now, today. My depression was pervasive, manifest in a terrible gnawing ache at the center of my being. It overwhelmed and beat me down. I had no strength left to fight for life, no desire for life because I felt powerless and foul and despicable, a rotten thing seeking solace in unconsciousness. It wasn't that I wanted to *die*—I simply wanted not to be.

The third time I returned to Westbrook Hospital, they gave me a series of shock treatments. They aren't painful, honestly, and at Westbrook they were almost considered a badge of merit—the little red sizzle marks on your brow where the clamps have been attached. The evening before, I was given an injection, a terrible parching medication to dry out my body and to prevent suffocation from saliva or vomit when the seizure hit. In the morning, long after the others had gone to breakfast, I lay in bed, waiting for the sound of the cart, the wobbly wheels that would carry the black box.

The small box is placed by my head, an injection of sodium pentathol administered, and as I begin to float away on waves of sedation, I am barely conscious of the arm and leg restraints and of the tongue depressor and . . . I awake with a crash! Miss Love says, "You've had a treatment,

146

*Carol. Stay quiet. I'll bring you some coffee and juice."
When she leaves, I finger my temples and feel the electric
abrasions there. I sleep. The electroshock is strange, but
not nearly so scary as Edith.*

Edith had not only had a lobotomy but occasionally
also had electroshock therapy. She was a big hulking
woman from a very wealthy family in the Midwest, and
she lived only to smoke cigarettes and eat candy. She
begged constantly for cigarettes and candy, in a gruff
monotone, and if you didn't give her some, she threatened
you with "frying." Edith could be pretty scary at times, but
our nurse, Miss Cordelia Love, had her well under control,
and I believe she cared deeply for Edith, almost as if she
were her own child.

Edith was a permanent resident of Oak Cottage, and
I was coming to fear that I would be one, too. That I was
going to be one of those people I had heard whispers about
as a child, people who visited home for short periods of
time but who really lived in insane asylums. When I said
this to my doctors, they nodded.

They sent me home.

*All around me the house creaks and murmurs. I clean up
the shards of our Thanksgiving dinner—a hurried meal
eaten in silence. Tom has left, gone off somewhere. I am
alone, scraping dishes, washing up. Outside, a drear November mists the kitchen window. I understand at last that
I am dying, that I have already died inside and only the
husk of me remains.*

*What I have to do is to stop the rest, the persistent
heart, the flickering brain, the lungs—autonomous parts of
me that only feed the pain and keep it going.*

147

*My little girls are asleep upstairs. I take my car keys,
my pills. "Tommy, Buck, take care of your sisters until
Daddy comes back. Please . . . take care."*

*The little boys look at me with round eyes. I cannot
look back at them; I cannot stop or think. I know only that
it has to finish. . . .*

*I know where to go. I have always known in the back
of my mind, seen it there, off the main road in a cluster of
trees. A tatty motel called the Manzel Bagh. The owners
had once lived in Persia and brought this improbable name
to backwoods Virginia. A desk clerk hands me a key. I pay
cash in advance. I park my car in the back, in the trees. In
the morning they will think that I have simply left—they
will not look for me.*

*Inside the musty room I walk straight to the bath-
room, fill a glass with water, take the pills. My heart is
beating fast, fast, thrumming in my ears. One handful
down, another . . . Librium, Seconal, Elavil, as many as
I've been able to hide. My hands are sweating. I lie on the
bed and light a cigarette. It will all be over soon; the black
void will overtake me.*

*I can feel it now, so fast, my limbs turning numb. Put
out the cigarette—don't start a fire!*

"God bless my children, take care of my children. . . ."

The state police found me. They insisted that Tom
walk into the room before them. In Virginia suicide is a
punishable offense. If they had been the ones actually to
discover me, they would have had to charge me with attempted murder. I think of Tom now, walking into that
airless room, think what he had to steel himself to discover
and of his courage. It was the convulsions that saved me—
violent seizures whose scars I carry to this day—scars on

my knees, a burn mark on my arm where it seems I extinguished my cigarette, and a puckered scar on my brow for all to see.

I came to in Intensive Care, in Richmond, the Saturday after Thanksgiving 1967. I opened my eyes to find Dr. Foster looking at me with the deepest sadness. "I won't," I said, "I promise I won't. I'll never do it again—I promise."

But it was too late, and, rightly, he didn't believe me. I was put in the women's locked ward for three months. No Miss Love, no porch, no strolls before lunch—no place to go *for* lunch. We were locked into our cells at night, unlocked in the morning. We ate our meals in the common room from trays—plastic forks, no knives. No belts, no scarves, no stockings. Nothing to do. No one to talk to. You see, everyone but me was mad. I was among babbling women, groaning women, women who laughed and screamed, autistic women who never moved once they had been put in place. Nothing changed day after day but the mushy menu.

I began playing games; I started joining the less hostile demented in their delusions. For the little old lady who called for taxis all day long, I played telephone, and sometimes taxicab, too. I went where she directed me, I tooted my horn. I bowed to the "Empress," and curtsied low, just as a visiting Rose Kennedy had taught us to at Noroton; for a full hour we'd had to listen to a very serious Mrs. Kennedy teaching us how to behave at court should we ever happen to visit Queen Elizabeth. One woman simply needed her head fondled; sometimes she banged it against the wall, like an infant in a crib. One of the nurses told me I had a talent for working with disturbed people, that perhaps I should become a psychiatric nurse. I hastened to inform her that when you are a disturbed person yourself, it comes naturally. "Doin' what comes naturally," that's what all my ward mates were doing. What the nurse was pointing out to me, and what I was unable to grasp at the time, was that some (healthy) part of me still connected with others and sought to soothe and care for them. The truly insane are impermeably locked inside themselves and exhibit only ritualized, mechanical behavior. Sometimes I felt as though I were living in a hive of bees.

I was transferred to Payne-Whitney in New York City. My old Noroton friend Martha Butler, now a psychiatric nurse, had convinced my family that Westbrook was not helping and that she believed Payne-Whitney might. Tom agreed. My friend Meredith, who had been released from the hospital the month before, drove me to the airport. She gave me stationery (with stamps already on the envelopes) and 711 cologne. When she hanged herself four months later, she left letters for Nancy and me. All she said really was "Good-bye, I'm sorry."

That Meredith committed suicide didn't surprise me. She had simply succeeded where I had failed. We mental patients knew about these things, we didn't have to talk about them. We knew about wanting and courting death, and so Meredith didn't have to explain anything to me, or to Nancy. She had only to tell us what she did: "Good-bye, I'm sorry."

By then I had become more hopeful. By then Dr. Herbert Rothman was leading me step by step into recovery. For beginners, he actually *talked*. I was taken off most of my medication and kept on a low dose of the antidepressant Tofranil. So when Dr. Rothman talked, I was able to listen and slowly, slowly, to understand. When I asked him questions, he answered. I learned about depression. I heard that it was a common response to loss. I got so that I could say that Maureen had died, but I could not talk about

Maureen—you see, if I had, I would have cried until there was nothing left. Just a puddle of me on the floor. We talked about dead babies, and my sister Allie. We talked a little about my father and about Mother, too.

I began dreaming and also remembering.

I am just learning to walk. I am in the Empire Room in Sharon, a long drawing room with heavy Empire furniture, formal and uncomfortable. Someone behind me sets me down on the floor and faces me toward my mother. There is a small push from behind, and I set off in the direction of her knees, a mighty wobble, listing from side to side, arms out for balance, arms out in the hope of being held. I feel I am walking in circles, balancing on air, but before I know it, arms flailing, I am there. I have reached my mother without falling; I hold tight to the silky material of her dress, I smell her perfume and hear her lilting laugh. There is applause from ladies in the room. And then I am picked up and taken away.

"You made it," said Dr. Rothman, "You made it to your mother's knees—made it all the way across the room."

"Yes, but then they took me away. . . ."

I remembered being put to bed in Sharon while it was still daylight, and my crib, and wallpaper flecked with tiny figures: lords and ladies, lambs, flying birds. My hands were bound in gauze and tape, apparently to prevent me from sucking my thumb. Every night I set about systematically biting off the bandages and then using my nails to scratch and peel at the wallpaper. By the end of the summer I had destroyed it, and my crib was moved to the other side of the room, set some feet away from the wall.

"You got the bandages off every night? You had the will to do that?"

What an optimist my doctor was! We talked about these memories, my psychiatrist and I. We spoke of my dreams. And of feelings. We talked about rage, the rage of little girls whisked away and of little girls with bound hands.

"Suicide," said Dr. Rothman, "is seldom an act of despair. It is far more likely to be an act of rage."

What an ugly word! What had rage to do with me? I am sweet, after all, generous, patient with friends. Good? I am good? I don't know where it turned around, when my badness and worthlessness began to fade, when I began to think I might have a chance at life. In August I was "presented" before the New York Hospital staff—seated on a platform to answer questions before a sea of white coats. They probed, I responded.

"What have you learned from your sister's death?" asks Dr. Whitecoat, the one with the pointy beard.

"That I would trade everyone in the world to have her alive—that I wish everyone else was dead."

Oh, oh . . .

I flunked, of course—Dr. Rothman told me that I had been dubbed a "psychiatric virgin." My release was put off for another month. I must have wised up fast, because in September of 1968 they sent me home. Only I didn't have a home. I knew only that I wouldn't be returning to Tom and to Do Well.

I spent some months at Great Elm in a house on the estate. My mother lived there alone now surrounded by her loyal servants. Jane lived nearby and also John and Jim and their families. My sister Priscilla visited on weekends.

Divorce was an ugly word in my family. I felt a pariah.

Mental illness, psychiatry—it wasn't what we *did*. And though my family never criticized me—in fact many of my brothers and sisters acted as though nothing had happened—I felt disloyal, self-conscious, aware on some level that I had let them down. To bring up my illness, or my suicide attempts, would have breached both good taste and my privacy. It would also have been embarrassing. For as a family we still didn't talk about those things, "personal" things. I, on the other hand, was learning that if I didn't speak them, I would drown again in depression.

Thanksgiving was approaching, the first anniversary of my suicide attempt. At the request of one of my sisters, my children and I had our turkey dinner at the White Hart Inn in the neighboring town of Salisbury. Our aging servants were often as overprotected as Mother herself. Having the children there might simply entail too much work. . . .

Ella telephoned me the next morning, wondering why I hadn't had Thanksgiving lunch at Great Elm "where you belong, little miss, with your family." I knew Ella had wanted me there, I knew and trusted Ella's heart. What I didn't know was whether anyone else had wanted me.

I had chosen Thanksgiving as the time to die: Thanksgiving, the essential family holiday, the time to feel most excluded, most alone within the confines of a family. It was not a conscious decision, of course, but then, the most meaningful choices seldom are. Thanksgiving is still difficult for me, still elicits feelings of anger and hurt even now that I understand why my sense of loneliness is so pervasive and acute. I was a "left out" child because I was born to be a baby when everyone else had grown up—as simple as that, as simple as chronology.

The only thing I understood from my Thanksgiving exclusion that first year after the hospitalizations was that

153

I didn't quite belong with the family. I simply had never become a full member, and not all the wishing in the world could make me one.

I would find a place to live and at least try again with my children. Make my own family. I could never change it for them—the year and a half of my disappearances and my wooden reappearances—but I could give them something good, at least from now on. I was prepared to give them everything, but you see, by then I had met Ray.

I am twenty-nine years old, the newly divorced mother of four little children, and I am alone. I meet him on a mellow September evening in New York City. I am wearing an emerald-green sleeveless dress and a mink stole about my shoulders. It is the color "autumn haze." I like my mink stole; it makes me feel sophisticated and smart.

"Are you cold?" he asks, teasing, his eyes alight.

Oh, he is handsome, beguiling. We go for drinks. I know immediately that he's the one—that he will be the one forever and ever. "I am so alone," I say to Ray. The words simply spill out. "Are you alone too?"

The needy woman I was then had to find a man. I didn't know women could be alone. I didn't think it was possible. The cushioned isolation of my life in Virginia had cut me off from the events of the 1960s: the civil rights marches, the antiwar demonstrations, and above all, the nascent women's movement. I struggled to catch up. I read Simone de Beauvoir's *The Second Sex* and found it "interesting." I sampled Susan Sontag. I read Betty Friedan, Germaine Greer, and Gloria Steinem, but having had so little exposure to people of my own age and generation, I still lived my mother's life, the life of another time cocooned in material comfort and female dependency.

Of course I would look to replace my husband. What else was there?

I moved to New York City and to Ray. New York is a wonderful place for lonely people, a haven for non-belongers. It is a city that takes you in, and it doesn't ask questions.

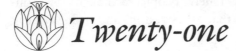 *Twenty-one*

Ray and I married in 1970. I had a new life. So did members of my family. My brother Bill had become a celebrity and could probably match his shoes and suits by now without anybody's help. It had begun in 1965 with his New York City mayoral race against John Lindsay and Abraham Beame. He ran with no intention, and no hope, of winning. He had volunteered himself in order to focus attention on, and elicit contributions to, the infant New York State Conservative Party. Bill made an engaging candidate, and he amused and titillated the media—he was eminently more quotable than candidates Lindsay and Beame. When asked by a reporter what he would do if he won the election, Bill answered, "I would demand a recount." And so began the transformation from conservative journalist and columnist to television personality. Comedians now imitated him on the Johnny Carson show; *Time* magazine put him on its cover.

Fame brings with it a great loss of privacy as one becomes hostage to the public fantasy. Bill would sacrifice a great deal for celebrity. It begins slowly, being recognized

Bill and Mother tangle with Bach at Bill's house in Stamford.

here, approached there. Personal time slips away in small increments, and soon there is almost none left. For you do not belong to yourself but to the people on the street who ask for autographs, the drunks on the plane who accost you, reporters, journalists. I seldom saw him now without a crowd of admirers (or detractors). His life was appointed to the minute, and so it was mostly on his sailboat, away

157

from the limelight and surrounded by close friends, that Bill was allowed simply to be himself.

My brother Jim had also attracted national attention. It was he who would next volunteer himself to the Conservative Party. He ran for the Senate from New York State in 1970, for Robert Kennedy's seat, which had been filled by the appointee Charles Goodell. Unlike Bill's candidacy for mayor, the senatorial campaign was a serious race, managed by the very competent Clifford White. Our old friend Marvin Liebman launched a fund-raising effort; Arthur Finkelstein took over the polling. Watching the candidates debate one night on television, my son Tommy burst into tears. We had just lost our little King Charles spaniel, Pompidou, and Tommy fled the room crying, "That man [Charles Goodell] looks just like Pompi!"

Goodell and Ottinger split the liberal vote between them, and the man I knew as my modest, shy brother went to Washington as United States Senator from New York. Jim's personality was the antithesis of a politician's; he retained an innocence on the job which, while it earned him the bemused respect of his fellow legislators, resulted in very few behind-the-scenes deals. Not for Jim the kind of old-boy networking and trading off that greases the wheels of Congress. He was a public servant first; he voted his principles, principles that did not always coincide with the interests of his constituents. The columnist Jack Anderson would call him the most diligent senator in the United States Senate.

That Christmas, after Jim's election, my sister Jane painted two signs and, after dark, staked them at either side of Jim and Ann's house in Sharon, Connecticut: "Welcome to New York State" and "You are now leaving New York State." The senator was not all that amused—his residency had been made a big issue during the campaign,

158

much as that of his predecessor, Senator Robert Kennedy, had been. By New Year's Day, the signs were down.

During the early seventies my mother's mind began its trajectory downhill. There were curious memory lapses and inappropriate responses. Her eyes dimmed, and she looked frightened and confused. She began to confabulate. And we, her children? Sometimes we pretended, too, denied her obvious senility. Sometimes we panicked and made the rounds of physicians who were themselves helpless to help. The woman I called Mother became more and more the child. The deaths of my sisters had made her so vulnerable that I was filled with an aching tenderness and grief for the person she had been, the person I saw dying in tiny increments.

The family "fortune" also declined. A large portion had been nationalized—those nervy Venezuelans taking back their oil! And a great portion of the money my father had left had been happily expended by his ten children and fifty grandchildren. At times the family business was helmless. My oldest brother, John, had retired, and Jim had left to become a senator, so Jane's oldest son, Cameron Smith, took over the day-to-day running of the company. But the big deals eluded us, and so, in the end, did the oil. Black gold was as frivolous and inconstant a mistress as our Father had always warned!

There were other changes at home as well: Kamschatka and Great Elm were becoming too costly to maintain. My mother had continued to live in both houses, with the servants growing as old and tottery as she. The moves north and south befuddled and confused her, and even the hiring of a companion did nothing to alleviate her anxiety. We felt she would be better in one place, perhaps in New York City, where the majority of her children lived and could visit her with more frequency.

159

We put Kamschatka up for sale and made plans to develop Great Elm, building apartments in the existing structures, and selling off lots of two to three acres, creating what is called a land association. It was a time of soaring interest rates, and the real estate market had come to a screeching halt. If we developed the estate ourselves, members of our family could remain there, owning at least a part of what had once been our home. The biggest wrench of all was to visualize Great Elm itself divided into five apartments, whole sections closed off and rooms vanished as if they had never been—especially the great dining room whose blue-papered walls had most certainly had ears.

The plans for Great Elm induced hysteria in some of the Sharon neighbors. Town meetings were called, and newcomers made their reputations by berating "the Buckleys." The local paper printed venomous letters. The controversy was covered by the *New York Times*. With Jim in the Senate and Bill a celebrity, our family seemed overnight to have become newsworthy. *Life* magazine had had us on its cover only a few years before: "The Buckleys: A Gifted American Family: The lovely old house speaks of the polished elegance of the large, talented, successful and politically conservative family whose home it is. Late last month the Buckleys—forty-seven of them— gathered at the estate of Great Elm in Sharon, Connecticut, to spend Thanksgiving and to celebrate together the family's latest triumph, the election of James L. Buckley as U.S. Senator from New York. . . . Aloise Steiner Buckley, a southern lady from New Orleans, still holds open house for her children. All are grown now and with children of their own, but they remain eager for a return to the sort of solidarity and mob intimacy that are part of going home again in a big family."

And yes, there is even a picture in the *Life* spread of Buckleys and Buckley grandchildren playing *touch football!* It was all very Kennedy. A period of trite comparisons began—two large, politically active Irish-American families—as uncomfortable for the Kennedy family, I'm sure, as for ours. For, in other ways, there are not two more disparate families than the Buckleys and the Kennedys. The Kennedys were trained for public service and for politics, and their fame and notoriety continued while ours whispered to a halt some time ago. We had not been brought up

New York's junior senator and family. Standing: *Jim, Priscilla, Carol, John, and Reid.* Seated: *Mother, Bill, and Jane.*

KHRUSHCHEV REMEMBERS
The Cuban Missile Crisis

THE BUCKLEYS
A Gifted American Family

The Buckleys at their
family home in Connecticut

DECEMBER 18 · 1970 · 50¢

to live in the public eye as they had. My father abhorred publicity.

Family legend has it that when my father first moved to Great Elm, a famed New York society columnist contacted him, saying that for a mere three hundred dollars a year he would mention at least one Buckley son or daughter in his column every month. My father wrote back and offered him three hundred dollars *never* to mention us. But the very public accomplishments of my brothers Jim and Bill had changed that, and so the feeding frenzy had begun about our plans for Great Elm.

What surprises you in a confrontation like the one over Great Elm is to find that people who you had thought were friends, are not. Not because they disagree with you but because of the vitriol they express—feelings of anger or envy that must have been suppressed for years. And so, once again, it was Buckleys against the world.

The atmosphere in the school auditorium reminds me of the only bullfight I have ever attended, makes me think of prizefights, of the breathy anticipation of blood about to spill. I am sitting next to my sisters Jane and Priscilla. Jane has taken the brunt of the town's hostility. She lives in Sharon full-time and has for most of her life. The uproar has hurt and surprised her most of all. My brother Jim and his wife, Ann, are also there. We sit stiffly in our chairs; we are embarrassed to be here, anxious about being in the spotlight and about the hostility that surrounds us.

The weekenders are here in droves, newcomers, and also some of our closest neighbors, ones who live in grand houses on our street. Our neighbors don't look at us; they look away. They aren't enjoying this as much as the new people.

A handsome doctor, a cookie-cutter man, blond and aquiline, takes the stage. He flushes with exhilaration, he walks up and down and orates, decries our disloyalty to the town, our poor taste, our willingness to destroy the neighborhood, our greed. Great Elm, he says, is easily salable. We haven't really tried; instead we plan to corrupt the town, to create a housing development! Why don't we just sell it? he cries. The auditorium goes wild with applause and whistles.

My brother Jim stands up, bows to the assembled in his courtly manner, and, stammering shyly, offers to sell Great Elm on the spot to the physician or to any of the assembled. With interest rates at fourteen percent, there aren't many people standing in line for mortgages.

There is silence, followed by scattered laughter here and there, applause. I have an impulse to reach out and squeeze my sister Jane's hand, but I don't. To do so would embarrass us.

The town meeting ends in an impasse. As we walk out, looking straight ahead, the townspeople, the working people in the town who have known our family for generations, reach out and take our hands and pat us diffidently on the arm, murmur words of encouragement.

The townspeople of Sharon supported us, working-class people whose families had lived there for the better part of the last century. They had fond memories of my father, affection for my mother, and respect for my two sisters, Priscilla and Jane. The family was liked, for, above all, we were polite, generous, seldom vindictive, even as we were oblivious to the anger and resentment we provoked in the weekenders and city folk.

Our family furniture, paintings, porcelain, silver, crystal, would be sold at auction. Even the old kitchen table, which used to be the playroom table and had some of my older siblings' initials carved into it. My three sisters—Priscilla, Jane, and Patricia—sat there together in Jeff and Ella's old pantry on the eve of the auction. The cavernous rooms of the big house had become a ghostly jumble of furniture, linens, housewares, and family possessions, on display for the viewing public. The kitchen was stark and lifeless, cabinets and drawers empty, Jeff's dusty old recliner pushed into a corner. We sat in straight chairs, elbows on the old playroom table, as my sisters reminisced, telling stories about their childhoods, laughing at times, remembering, avoiding our tomorrow. We were seldom together like this, the four remaining sisters, seldom together and relaxed and reflective. I felt close to them, hearing a family history that I had never experienced.

They remembered their early years living in the château in Chantilly, just outside of Paris. There was a large pond there with nasty swans that bit. Once they deliberately tipped over a boat bearing a portly visiting priest and then had to drag him ashore, all floating black robes.

They spoke of the family move to London and of their Spartan English boarding schools and of trading puddings to their fellow students for baths and hair-washes; Americans at that time were considered bizarrely hygienic. They got chilblains and fine educations and developed the unusual accent that marks my family's speech. Jimmy was caned, and it was that incident that finally convinced my parents to liberate the children and to return to the United States, to the schoolhouse on Great Elm, and to preparatory schools and colleges.

My sisters told me about "the incident." This family crisis had only been referred to as "the incident." It was never discussed in my father's presence, and Mother looked pained and hurt at its very mention. To my young mind, this was a dark family secret. Not even Allie had talked about it. What a disappointment it turned out to be!

My three sisters—Priscilla, Jane, and Patricia—and two school friends, bored stiff one winter evening in Sharon (the house was officially closed for the winter) and inspired by the much publicized prank of some Princeton boys, decided in like manner to torment Dr. Cotter. Dr. Cotter was the Episcopalian minister, and we Buckleys considered him exceedingly stuffy and righteous. Dr. Cotter may not have been as stuffy as we supposed, however, for his two daughters were later to become the talented comediennes Jayne and Audrey Meadows.

The five girls, my sisters among them, climbed giggling through a window into the church, spread honey on the pulpit and pews, and placed *New Yorker* and *Esquire* illustrations in the prayer books, joyously anticipating the shocked response of Mr. Cotter's parishioners on the following Sunday morning. What a wonderful prank! What fun! How pleased they were with their cleverness and guile!

Not. Within days, their arrests made headlines in the *Daily News* and *New York Herald Tribune*. The local paper, the *Lakeville Journal,* described the police investigation thus: "There was an absence of clews [*sic*] to the pranksters, but State Policeman Donald Frost reasoned that not many residents possessed the magazines involved and he started unraveling the mystery from this point." And yes, not only were the incriminating magazines discovered at Great Elm but also a suspect honey jar.

Officer Frost, having unraveled the mystery, was dispatched to Nightingale-Bamford School in New York to "detain for questioning" my sister Patricia—had he known Trish, he wouldn't have wasted his time. There is no one more stubbornly loyal than my sister Patricia. She refused to name her two cohorts, and thus my sisters were left to take the rap. Our outraged father refused to speak to them or ever to refer to "the incident" again, and Mother was left tearfully to pay the fine—"$100 Each"—and to fend off the disapproving stares of our fine neighbors.

I listened to my sisters' stories, enthralled. I discovered that Jimmy had been a wild child and Billy, delicate and frail, and John, the recipient of a Purple Heart. He had, he said, injured his knee in North Africa while ducking under a Jeep to avoid enemy fire. It is quite likely that John performed an act of courage during the war; it is just as likely that he made up this story out of whole cloth. I believe the war had more effect on John than his stories revealed, but he would continue through life to avoid distress by making fun and making light.

Days after the Normandy invasion, John and a muddy, exhausted cadre of young soldiers approached a newly liberated French farmer and asked him for a bottle of Calvados. He refused. They offered him army scrip in payment. He refused. They offered him American cigarettes.

"Je ne fume pas," he answered curtly.

Exasperated, thirsty, John unstrapped his pistol and, holding it to the farmer's head, said: *"De cet instant, monsieur, vous êtes fumeur!"* (From this moment, sir, you are a smoker!) The boys got their Calvados.

And so we were auctioning off memories, a family history, an era, a time that I had been born too late to share in. I made the mistake of walking through the big house the following day, mingling with the auction preview crowd. An old chair from Mademoiselle's room with the stuffing falling out had been brought down from the third floor. "Phew," said a woman in a sequined T-shirt. "Disgusting! Wouldn't you think they'd know better?"

❀ *Twenty-two*

Six years had passed since I moved to Manhattan. Jim was now up for reelection; Bill had become a best-selling author of spy novels and moderated his own television discussion show, *Firing Line*. But what was much more important to me than any of this was my new life and my marriage to Ray.

We had been married these six years—intensely. It was all passion: love, anger, disappointment, hurt, and reconciliation. He was my soul mate, my other half, endearing, intriguing, filling me with his love, and then— like that!—taking it away again. To the world we appeared an infatuated couple. But behind closed doors there were things I never spoke about. Hostile rages that seemed to come from nowhere, furious explosions I prayed my children wouldn't hear, words spoken aloud that I had never heard used before. I had no experience of this kind of anger, and it filled me with panic, sent me searching frantically for what it was I had done to provoke it. But part of my punishment was not to be told: I should have *known*; if I truly loved him I would have known. And so I guessed, spent the years of our marriage guessing.

Often, when faced with his white rage, I would call to mind the somber, unsmiling child in the black-and-white photos his mother had shown me. I saw the man in the child, and the child in Ray: the four-year-old boy torn away from his secure and comfortable home in Luxembourg, shepherded through Vichy France by his frantic parents. They were on their way to Portugal and to a ship there that would accept Jews—there were many ships that would not—and carry them to safety and to the United States. Along the way, his mother would take from him his favorite pillow, for if the Nazis were to discover them, the pillow would certainly go—and much, much more.

"He should get used to it now," she explained.

She told me that once, very close to their destination, Ray left his toy soldier collection on a train. He screamed out his loss and anger until they found it again—he screamed and kicked like a normal little boy, his cries reverberating up and down the station platform where there were always Germans on the lookout for escaping Jews. Miraculously, they escaped detection.

Ray's mother smiles incredulously as she tells me this: "And one year later in New York City, what did he do? He gave away his toy soldiers to a boy in school for a baseball mitt. A baseball mitt!" No, she says, she will never understand it.

I can. I can believe the power of a child's need to belong. Ray would always trade his toy soldiers for baseball mitts, and I think part of his rage came from having to do so, from having to yearn and work so hard for acceptance by a foreign, and often hostile, culture. He learned early what it was to be an outsider and a Jew—the Irish kids in Washington Heights taught him well. He worked hard, excelled, was accepted at Stuyvesant High School, one of New York's special schools for gifted students. At fifteen he entered the Wharton School at the University of Pennsylvania.

An American success story. But success seldom heals early wounds. I knew that. For though I myself now felt well, happy, and successful, inside, a lonely, abandoned child waited patiently to be hurt and to be left.

Our children heard our fights, of course. One evening my stepdaughter, Dawn, and Tommy and Buckley ran away, left our house in Sharon and walked the two miles to Great Elm in the dark, rolling up in blankets by the pool. For the whole night. To teach us a lesson and stop us from fighting. One night Ray left me at a party and locked me out of the apartment. One night I ran away too, leaving the Sharon house for a motel room.

But none of this matters. It will go away. The anger and the outbursts will stop, for I love him enough to make them stop. I adore him. He will finally come to believe and to trust in my love for him. This is the man who gives me belief in myself, a little anyway—I see it reflected in his eyes. I still feel about him as I did when first we met. I need him—without him I feel that I barely exist. I am everything he wants me to be. I hope I am . . . I strive to be.

Ray had made a great success of his business since our marriage. He had established his own trading company, buying and selling agricultural chemicals around the world. He was talented, intelligent, and courageous enough to take the risks that success demands. He was flush with his good fortune, and we moved from my apartment on Seventy-third and Lexington to 765 Park—a lofty twelve-room apartment wrapped around the corner of Park Avenue and Seventy-second Street. We had by now melded his two children and my four, somewhat successfully. His daughter, Dawn, and I were never to resolve our difficulties, for I was the woman who had stolen away her father. And in case I hadn't fully understood, Dawn bought her father a book one Christmas titled *The Man Who Got Away*.

She was a spirited girl, histrionic, willful, a child hungry for her father, a child who seemed to resent me and mine as intruders and as a threat to her relationship with him even as she yearned to belong. Her brother, Serge, six years younger than she, was an affectionate, intense little boy, wise beyond his years. And while Serge was given to earthshaking tantrums whenever his will was crossed, he cared for us, loved us as his family. My children felt alienated by Dawn, but Serge they accepted as their baby brother.

Our Judeo-Christian ménage worked, Christmas and Passover were observed. Religion had never been an issue between Ray and me, and if my brothers and sisters were saddened by my own defection from the Catholic church, they in no way held Ray responsible. In fact, they welcomed him to the family, grateful for the seeming happiness and stability he had brought me.

Of all of our children, little Serge especially loved Christmas, and the putting out of our little wooden crèche filled him with almost unbearable excitement, for the crèche meant that Santa and his mounds of toys were not far behind.

"Mother," says six-year-old Serge, "what does it mean that you're a Christian and I'm a Jew?"

170

He watches as I place the tiny carved figures on the mantel: Joseph, Mary, the baby Jesus, and some outrageously misproportioned camels, sheep, and shepherds. No kings. I had purchased the crèche in Bethlehem, from an Arab selling souvenirs near the Church of the Nativity.

"Well . . ." I pause, giving myself time to think, to discuss the matter both ecumenically and in the simplest way possible. . . .

"Tell me, tell me, what does it mean?" Patience is not one of Serge's qualities.

"Well, Serge, you see, Jesus was born a Jew but he . . ."

"So . . . ?"

"Hush, Serge, listen to me: Jesus was believed to be the Messiah, and so some Jews believed he was the Messiah, the Son of God, and others didn't. And the ones who did became Christians, and the ones who didn't stayed Jews."

"And . . ."

"Well, it all became very angry—the discussion about who was God and who wasn't. And for years and years there was fighting and persecution, and it wasn't what Jesus would have wanted at all."

"So?"

"So, Serge, now things are better. You see, we're a Jewish and Christian family, and we get along. And Christmas is Jesus's birthday . . ."

"Wait-a-minute, wait-a-minute, wait-a-minute . . ."

"Yes, Sergie?"

"You mean the fight is about who is God?"

"Well, yes."

"You know what I think, Mother?" He gives me a knowing look. "I think Christians and Jews should still be fighting. . . ."

And so we had plenty, Ray and I. We had a family, we had a pretty eighteenth-century house in Sharon, we had a Colombian maid; we had everything, a Saab and a station wagon *and* a convertible. But everything was not enough. There was a world of baseball mitts out there, and the new one for Ray was collecting art.

He had a fine and growing collection; it was eclectic, aesthetically pleasing, and sometimes humorous as well. It ranged from a delicate Boucher oil, *The Milk-Maid,* to Tamara de Lempica portraits of the Deco-rich and jaded. He owned two Burchfields, three Elie Nadelman sculptures. He collected drawings by Bouchardon and Charles Le Brun and Tiepolo and limited-edition leather-bound folios illustrated by Matisse, by Picasso and Miró. He had a small Pissarro pastel, a Joseph Cornell shadow box, a Morris Kantor, a Nevelson, a Marsh, a Lipchitz, a Soyer, a Walkowitz, a Stoors pen-and-ink . . . The list went on. And the collecting would go on. The collection would become more current, more with-it, more Mary Boone—much more current and with-it than I would ever be able to be. The collecting would begin to give him something I never could.

In October of 1975 I had planned the ultimate surprise party to celebrate Ray's fortieth birthday. I had told a hundred lies to put this party on. Most of them, of course, to Ray. I had sent top-secret memos to our guests, hung around the Plaza Hotel engaging carriage drivers, ordered the wines and cake sculpted in icing to look exactly like the S.S. *France,* Ray's favorite ship and the last of the great ocean liners. I hurried and cajoled the painters in the new apartment to finish. The Park Avenue apartment had just been renovated, though we would not move into it for another month. The dining room walls were shellacked a deep raspberry, the library walls covered in hunter-green felt with bookcases painted a Chinese red. Asprey's would furnish it with Brighton Pavilion cane chairs and a leather sofa. We bought burgundy and gold porcelain there as well. The foyer was done in black and white tiles; there were four fireplaces, and so many closets that one was reserved exclusively for firewood and one for our cases of wine. Those, the two of us set about seriously to deplete.

I apologized to Ray, saying that we must put off his birthday celebration because Bill and my sister-in-law, Pat, were holding a fund-raising cocktail party for Jim. Jim's Senate reelection campaign against Daniel Patrick Moynihan was heating up. "Rats," I said to my husband, "we have to wear evening clothes, and just for drinks!" Could we just stop by the new apartment, though, where Ray's present had been delivered? I wanted him to have at least that before walking over to Bill's. Oh, I was excited!

I haven't forgotten his face, or the laughter and affection expressed that evening. Ray unlocked the door to the brand-new foyer and sauntered in, very elegant in his tuxedo. In seconds, doors flew open from every side to reveal my brother John, Priscilla, Jim and Ann, Bill and Pat, Reid and Tasa, flown up from South Carolina, Gerry and his wife, Seton, Shep Raimi, an old friend, my beloved quixotic Marvin Liebman, our friends the Hoags, the Durkins, the Weils, Howard Eliot, and the children. They had ginger ale and grape juice while the rest of us had either champagne and caviar or chilled vodka and caviar.

I have set up the bar on sawhorses, and as the chandeliers and lighting fixtures are not yet in place, there are candles everywhere. We drink and toast and drink and open presents. Lined up on Seventy-second Street are the eight carriages I have commandeered from Central Park. They transport our by now hilarious party to the 21 Club, though spoilsports Pat and Marvin hail a cab; Pat and Marvin are not buggy-ride types. At 21, in a private dining room, our party resumes. I am wearing the shimmering Zandra Rhodes that Ray bought for me in London, last trip over. I am flushed with happiness, I am delighted and also relieved that all has gone as planned. After dinner, after the Greenberg cake has been cut, Lisa Benkhert, a beautiful Upper East Side matron whom I had "purchased" at a charity auction, belly-dances in and wraps her scarf around Ray's head and shoulders. He blushes.

Twenty-three

*W*e breathed each other's air, Ray and I, and the children stood by and watched and grew tall. There were trips abroad two or three times a year: Ray and I in Singapore, at the Plaza-Athénée in Paris, Ray and I living just like my mother and father, traveling like them, in love like them, glamorous like them. Ray and I at the apartment he purchased in Cannes. Ray and I at Claridge's, in Luxembourg, visiting his mother there, restoring a house that we would never live in. Ray and I in Rome, in Senegal, in Israel, Pakistan, India . . .

We arrived in Delhi on the brink of the 1971 India-Pakistan War. There were rumors that the shining dome of the legendary Taj Mahal was to be covered in camouflage to prevent a bombing by the Pakistanis. As soon as we could, we drove to Agra, children and farm animals flying from beneath the wheels of our speeding, honking taxi. Once there, we hired a private guide, a wizened Indian gentleman in hand-me-down British tweeds and hand-me-down manners. He bowed and puffed, courtly and magnanimous, plying us with quantities of fruit juice·and sticky

175

candy; he guided us from room to room and, in his clipped Raj accent, described the wonders of the Taj as it must have been. After mounting a parapet to look across the river in order to view the site of the never-completed Black Taj, we paused to light cigarettes. Ray and I looked over the river, a sluggish mud-brown stream winding below. I saw a sheep, or was it a cow? Some bloated gray object floating in the water.

I looked again. It was a body—a human being. I turned to the guide. "Someone has drowned," I said. "We must call the police, the authorities!"

His brown face deepened a shade, and then with a little bow, half deference, half deprecation, he answered, "Ah, you see it is the humble people, the peasants," I think he was proud to use this term—a word we Westerners might understand. "They are ignorant, you see, and so"—he hunched his shoulders—"they dispose of their dead like so. . . ."

Like so . . . like India. When next he reached for my hand, to help me down a step, I had to force myself to be touched by him. I felt nauseated. The children in Bombay and Delhi chased us everywhere. "Mama," they cried, "mama." One girl child carried her infant brother, his two blind blue orbs staring into the sun. Our Indian hosts hurried to remind us that begging is after all a profession in India. "Probably they blinded the baby deliberately, hoping you will give them more money. You see?"

I was horrified. In India whole families slept on the streets; in Brazil wild boys ripped gold chains off your neck. I was shocked and angered. Savage places, these! In New York, in the ensuing years, we would experience both phenomena. Would we adapt like the Indians and the Brazilians and look away? Surely not, not in America . . .

176

Ray is taking me to Bermuda to celebrate my fortieth birthday. "No beautiful woman should become forty in her own hometown!"

I am pleased, of course, touched at his thoughtfulness, but also—well, a little hurt. For I am the great occasion party-giver! Over the years I have given ten—fifteen?—grand and elaborate surprise parties for the people I love. And I had thought (it had crossed my mind) that someone might be doing the same for me. I am, after all, going to be forty.

My sisters call and wish me a happy birthday; some of my friends take me out for lunch. Reid calls and asks me exactly when my birthday is. I can't believe he still doesn't know!

On a bright November morning we rush to La Guardia—with Ray it is always a rush where airports are concerned—and no sooner do we enter the terminal than he takes me by the shoulder and rushes me toward a bank, mumbling, "We have to change some money."

Money! Change money to go to Bermuda?

I need cigarettes and leave him looking harried and confused as the bank teller wonders aloud, "Change money for Bermuda, sir?" I find a newsstand. There, browsing through the paperbacks, I see my brother Reid. To my left is his wife, Tasa!

"Reid! Tasa! I can't believe it. What are you doing here?"

"I have a lecture in Indianapolis. And you? Oh, of course, you're on your way to Bermuda. Happy birthday, Carolita!" It seems my brother is giving me an awfully long hug—in fact, he doesn't seem to want to let me go.

But wonder of wonders, as I finally pull free, there stands my sister Priscilla—her back to me, perusing the candy counter! Priscilla, who never eats candy . . .

177

"Hi," she says blushing, "I'm on my way to Camden. To go dove shooting. To visit Polly Sheffield. To go to the races . . ." This is my sister Priscilla who was once trained to work as a spy for the CIA. I'm relieved for the CIA that she has changed professions, for she seems terribly flustered and her face is beet red.

"Bye," they cry suddenly, "bye-bye," and take off, racing in different directions.

Ray rounds the corner, winded, as if he'd run a ten-minute mile.

"Ray, you won't believe this, but I just ran into—"

"Later, later," he says. "Tell me later. Can't you see we're late for the plane?"

"But—"

Then, with both hands on my shoulders, he skids to a stop and wheels me around a good ninety degrees, panting: "Coffee—we have to have coffee." The gate temporarily forgotten, I am pushed into the coffee shop.

"We're late, but we have time for coffee," he says, sliding me into a booth.

I sit, but not before . . .

"Oh, Ray, you won't believe this. I must be having hallucinations—I swear that was Bill and Pat racing toward the—"

"Nope. It must be middle age. You're forty years old; you need glasses. Drink your coffee." My husband is acting very strange. My husband is very confused.

The loudspeaker crackles a last call, and now we race in earnest, Ray pulling me down the wobbly gangplank, for it seems the airplane doors will surely shut us out. "Please," Ray shouts at the flight attendant, "please, we have tickets—don't shut the doors!"

We stumble in just in time, carry-ons slapping at our

sides. I have a stitch in my side and an enormous resent-
ment against my discombobulated, disorganized husband.
Is he mad?

Not mad, my Ray, just a dissembler. For there they
are—an entire first-class section filled with pink-cheeked
Buckleys, laughing, clapping, cheering—all en route to Ber-
muda to celebrate baby's fortieth birthday.

Sometimes the children accompanied us on our trips.
Ray thought they should at least once experience a trans-
atlantic crossing. In many ways he was like my father—generous, imaginative, and wanting his children to have all the
things he hadn't had himself as a youngster. He booked pas-
sage aboard the second-to-last voyage of the SS *France*. One
cabin for the girls—Dawn, Anne, and Carol; one cabin for
the boys—Tommy, Buckley, and Serge; and a cabin for us.

Dressing for dinner provoked nightly crises. Dawn lost
her dress shoes and the top button of her one good blouse,
Carol had no clean underpants—none, she said. Anne had
one white sock, one blue, and one in between. Tommy and
Buckley resisted neckties, or pretended to be lost on board,
and Serge had tantrums. Everywhere. Serge had so many
tantrums he was expelled from the gym area, from the
Ping-Pong area, from the shuffleboard area, and finally
from the movie theater. Somehow, I wasn't handling this
crossing as well as my mother had in years past. I don't
recall her riffling through suitcases in search of missing
socks and underpants, I don't recall her requesting all-
points bulletins over the loudspeaker system in search of
missing miscreant children.

Tommy, who developed a taste for crêpes Suzette,
ordered them for dessert after every dinner—I think what
he liked was to see them made. The wait, however, as

Ray and I and our unruly crew aboard the SS France. From left to right: *Dawn, Tom, Anne, Ray, Carol Sr., Carol Jr., Serge, Buckley.*

the steward melted butter, added brandy, and flambéed the crêpes, was intolerable for the younger children, in particular Serge, and inevitably one or two left the table in a sulk (Anne and Carol) or in a tantrum (Serge). Dawn, who, gritting her teeth, called me "Mother" at that time, said one evening: "You drink too much, Mother. Maybe you're an alcoholic?"

A what? I drank like everyone else, one of the last generation of devoted martini aficionados. I had a couple of glasses of wine at lunch, a couple of cocktails before dinner, and couple of glasses of wine with dinner, and a couple of *digestifs* after, appropriately sipped with a porcelain demitasse of hot black coffee. A couple here, a couple there. Did that make an alcoholic? Alcoholics lied, hid bottles, drank in the morning, and got the shakes. Poor Dawn, here was just another example of her overactive imagination.

One October, Ray and I found ourselves aboard the

180

QE2 with Bill and Pat. The ship had been chartered by an entrepreneur, John Shaheen, to transport his guests to Newfoundland for the opening of his oil refinery there. He had plans also to publish a New York newspaper, and so the voyage included both business associates (Ray) and journalists (Bill). We had fun, lots of laughs, eating, drinking, gambling at night in the casino. It was a lazy, luxuriant journey, punctuated only by the ship's bulletins which, like an ongoing soap opera, relayed news of the day-by-day leaks in the Watergate affair. It was the beginning of the Saturday night massacre, and as fast as Bill had typed one column, he had to amend it or to begin again: Archibald Cox, Elliot Richardson, Ruckelshaus, Bork—one by one they tumbled.

Otherwise there was nothing to do but to be catered to. One night at dinner, Ray asked for a second serving of caviar.

"Now, now, sir," said the perky waiter, "it doesn't do to be piggy, does it?" as generations of Cunard stewards rolled in their graves.

The travelogue continued, a glamorous life as brisk and bright as the snaps from a Polaroid camera. And it was fun, of course, if a little frantic sometimes, but it is the quiet, ordinary days of our marriage that I remember best and hold dear.

Mornings in our Sharon house. It is always deep summer, and though my bedroom windows are shaded by giant maples in front, the still air banked against the screens is already heavy with the midday heat to come. I slumber, awake and not awake, hearing and not hearing the sounds of my house and family. Serge, up even before his father, is making accident-on-purpose noises in order to wake his brothers and sisters and alleviate his boredom. But Tommy and Buckley, sluggish in their early puberty, have learned to ignore all intrusions, pillows over heads, bodies heavily inert. Tommy and Buckley, hair tousled, will make it downstairs just in time for lunch. And then they have plans, serious plans that involve fishing, swimming, hanging out with their buddies, and possibly smoking dope.

The kitchen begins to resonate with small voices, Anne and Carol looking in cupboards for food, Dawn ordering the day, and everybody telling Serge to be quiet, go away. The kitchen door opens: Daddy, back from town with paper bags filled with groceries we do not need, and newspapers, and energy. "Daddy, can I have . . . Daddy, can I have . . ." and before Ray unpacks his parcels, I hear his footsteps, smell the fresh coffee he is bringing me, and the paper. "Hi," I say, sleepily, "thanks."

"Hi," he whispers. " 'Morning."

Pandemonium below and pungent smells of Ray's culinary efforts: scrambled eggs and salami, toaster waffles, burning bagels, cream cheese, and of course, the half grapefruit for Serge. No one knows how it came to be that Serge requires a half grapefruit. The rest of us don't have to have half grapefruits; Ray doesn't make himself a half grapefruit. Maybe Serge is prone to rickets? Whatever, what began as a treat has now become an insult, and Serge and his father will engage in endless grapefruit confrontations.

My decadent slumber ends in a cacophony of clumps, for this is the summer of the clog. Dawn, Anne, and Carol wear only clogs, clunking them up and down the uncarpeted stairs and across the wide board floors of our colonial house. "Mother!" "Mommy!" "Mom!"

Yes, yes . . . They cluster around my bed, sparkling

with life and with demands, half dressed, some T-shirted,
one shorted. Nothing matches—pink stripes with yellow
gingham, jean shorts and a bathing suit top. "Can we? Can
we?" Oh, they have plans for the day and sometimes for
the evening as well. For Dawn is our family innovator: she
is planning a play. Dawn is director, producer, choreogra-
pher, and star. Carol has been allotted the role of ticket-
taker, one dollar per guest; Anne is understudy and
invitation-maker. Can I call and invite their grandmother,
Mimi, and Aunt Jane and Aunt Pitts? Will Aunt Ann and
Uncle Jim come? Uncle John? And their cousins Jennifer
and Susie?

Yes and yes and yes. I dress quickly, throw on jeans
and a T-shirt, sandals. I carry the empty mug downstairs,
and there is Ray, seated at last at the kitchen table, a mug
of coffee half full at his side, the New York Times *and the*
Wall Street Journal *spread haphazardly among bagel*
crumbs, jam, juice cartons, and in splendid isolation at the
foot of the table, Serge's untouched half grapefruit.

The sink is filled with greasy plates, the counters spill-
ing over with half-emptied grocery bags, and the floor,
washed just last night, is sticky. Good morning, Carol! The
day begins for me, the cleaning up, the trips to town, the
marketing, the pool-sitting, the laundry, the telephone
calls, the games, the mediations, negotiations—the long,
hot, happy summer day.

I put my arm around my husband's shoulder, brush
my cheek against his. The softness of his skin always takes
me by surprise. "The girls are putting on another play
tonight."

"Did Serge," he says, "did Serge run away without
finishing his grapefruit?" We look down the table in silence

183

*at the noble grapefruit, held just so in a white china bowl,
its perfect pink sections unmarred, glistening in the morning light.*

*A bloodcurdling scream from upstairs and the mo-
ment slips away.* Clump-clump-clump, slam-bang—*Dawn
marches outraged into the kitchen: "Beau peed in my bed!"*

*And he has. Anne's cat, Beau, has definitely peed in
Dawn's bed.*

*"I think," I say, whispering into Ray's ear, "I think
this evening's production may be off after all."*

In New York, the tempo of our days was changing.
Three of the children were now away at school, and the
apartment loomed large and empty without them. There
was party-giving and party-going. In New York in the seventies we seldom gave dinner parties for just friends or for
people who knew each other or even for people *you* knew.
Often the Whitney Museum, on whose board Ray now
served, sent over a list—and we entertained it. "It" always
included at least one famous person: sometimes you got
Louise Nevelson, replete with mink eyelashes; sometimes
you got James Rosenquist. Ms. Nevelson held court,
perched at one end of the raspberry velvet sofa, nodding at
the obsequious guests and looking bored. James Rosenquist carried a dog biscuit and gnawed on it. Do you suppose he was giving up smoking?

My brother Jim's Senate fund-raising staff also sent
lists. Once we had Senator Orrin Hatch and once, Henry
Kissinger. Dr. Kissinger gave us a sonorous foreign policy
speech over drinks while Beau, our cat, paraded up and
down the coffee table behind his back, nibbling daintily on
the hors d'oeuvres. A tall, impassive Asian gate-crashed the
party and attached himself like glue to the guest of honor.

184

We discovered later that he was editor-in-chief of the Reverend Moon's newspaper, and we never did learn why he wanted to see Dr. Kissinger.

I played Perle Mesta, though it wasn't a life I understood, and no matter how elegant the actual party, I was always frantic beforehand, anxious about the food, the service; anxious that I would do or say something to make Ray angry. I felt accountable for things beyond my control and for things I couldn't anticipate. It has taken time and distance for me to understand that his rages had little to do with me, that they came from an earlier time and were rooted in the chaos of his childhood. I was simply *there* when the anger happened. I was convenient and I responded in a satisfactory manner—abjectly and with panic, for there was a part of me so filled with need of him that I could not separate myself from his attacks.

What did upset him was my lack of interest in society, or what passed for society. I think that he would never understand my own shyness, my own insecurities, my discomfort in large gatherings. And yet it was that very part of me that had attracted him, the uncertain child I was. Underneath the polish, the southern manners and grace that I exhibited so facilely, we were the same, he and I, outcasts drawn together by the shared experience of isolation.

He sensed, too, but couldn't understand my ambivalence about the luxurious life he had provided me. It was what he had thought I needed and wanted, a life that reflected my childhood. But times had changed, "status" had arrived, and our existence now centered on how things looked, how I looked (which took money and constant maintenance), how the apartment looked, and the walls and the art on the walls. The homes my parents had created had been created for their family, for friends, even four-legged ones. This Park Avenue creation was made for the world to see—it exuded wall-to-wall money. I felt no sense of friendship from most of the people we entertained, and the children couldn't feel at home there, were not made to feel at home. Museums are like that: Careful! Watch where you go, tread softly, whisper. . . . This was not the home I had envisioned, the sanctuary I had wanted for my uprooted children.

There was also a stultifying uniformity to the life, for all of the moneyed New York matrons sought, above all, to look like . . . moneyed New York matrons. We used the same caterers—in those days it was Glorious Foods. If the Schiffs across the street were giving a dinner party the week after yours, you'd check with Shaun Driscoll to make sure you weren't ordering any of the same courses. We met at the same hairdresser, the same aerobics class, the same benefits. And at each meeting we said the same things. Being friends was not really a part of the drill. It was a strange, insular existence, locked in by status and externals. And it was hard work and required constant attention—the effort to keep up, keep the skirts long or short or mid-calf, appear at the right restaurants, say the right (clever) things.

I was beginning to feel inept again and unsure. My husband's anger was always at the edge of our relationship, just there, waiting. . . . I could never rest with rage just around the corner; I had always to be ready for it. The only protection I understood was to withdraw into my books, to withdraw and to drink. A little buzz every night goes a long away. It blurs—it lets you pretend.

And then there were the committees. By 1978 I served on five boards of directors. The work on these not-for-profit boards involved meeting too often, voting on incomprehensible annual budgets, the projected and actual ones of which never matched, and fund-raising. Now, fund-raising, at least for the female board members, meant: giving parties. I had joined the boards, one, because I had never learned to say no, and, two, because remembering my Sacred Heart mentors, I felt the need to give back, to return some of what I had been given. Instead of good works, however, I seemed to be giving parties again. More parties . . .

It is ten o'clock on a weekday morning somewhere in Manhattan. Twelve women and maybe four men sit around a table. There are stacks of Xerox copies in front of each seat: president's reports, treasurer's reports, minutes of the last meeting, fund-raising reports, special-events reports, nominating committee reports. The men are gray and businesslike—there are fewer of them but they talk more. The women, early to late middle age, are uniformed: caps of blondish hair done by Kenneth or by M. Marc, bright polished nails, big gold earrings, slender gold chains, Cartier watches, silk blouses, Adolfo suits (Nancy Reagan is first lady), panty hose, heels. And hangovers.

When the board meetings are held in the mornings you can definitely recognize the hangovers—puffy eyelids, stale breath, catarrh, and in some of the extreme cases, tiny hand tremors. We all started out attractive and have ended up strained, little creases and etched lines, set mouths that not all the Elizabeth Arden facials in the world can erase. And we are the lucky ones, the kept women, women with nothing and everything to do. We run these charities as competently as the board of General Motors runs General

Upper East Side matrons conspiring to part you from your money. Standing: Pat Buckley and Tish Baldrige. Seated: Lady Jeanne Campbell and a bouffant author.

Motors, but we don't feel competent, for we are the last generation of do-nothing women. "Homemakers"—that is what our passports say on the line that says "profession."

We are nice, and only criticize each other behind each other's backs. But to tell the truth, we don't even do very much of that. For one, we are too busy; for two, we know about each other, understand, even without speaking, life's disappointments, life's traps: her husband plays around, hers drinks, hers hits when he's angry; the kids take drugs, flunk out of school, get pregnant, talk back. We don't have to say these things to each other; we know and, knowing, feel close. In that way we are more fortunate than men; in that way we are also more burdened. Today, this morning,

*each one of us hopes not to serve on the benefit committee;
today each one of us will volunteer.*

I chaired an auction for the Convent of the Sacred
Heart. I procured donations of a ride on the Goodyear
blimp, a personal tour of the White House, a luxury trip to
Beirut (the war in Lebanon erupted six weeks later). I in-
veigled my brother Bill and Norman Mailer to volunteer as
guest auctioneers. They weren't as adept as William Doyle
at actually selling the items, but they were high-spirited
and witty and entertained the guests.

My friend Mary Durkin and I gave a celebrity back-
gammon party at Doubles to raise money for Jim's reelection campaign. After dinner, guests bid for celebrity
partners. All the gentlemen who challenged Dina Merrill
lost their shirts for the sheer joy of simply gazing at her. We
made a lot of money for the campaign that night. Barbara
Healy and Mary and I arranged a whistle-stop train tour
for the campaign. The train was only a little more depressed than Buffalo and Syracuse, just about as run-down
and bleak, but we had fun, and so I believe did the candidate—one of the last fun times of the campaign.

A few weeks later, as the *Daily News* poll had pre-
dicted, Daniel Patrick Moynihan took the vote and became
our next U.S. Senator. Mary Durkin and I had organized a
Buckley victory party at the Waldorf. By nine o'clock it
was over—and the band had taken a break! Mary ran to
Mike Carney to ask him to begin playing, anything to lift
the pall that had settled on the assembled as CBS, NBC,
and ABC relayed our defeat at the polls. The band played
"Happy Days Are Here Again!"

We were sad; some staff members were bewildered
and shocked. A campaign is like a Broadway opening—we

fed on one another's enthusiasm, looked to each other for encouragement—and so were not adequately prepared for the lousy reviews next morning.

I chaired a fashion show at the Plaza, and the Estée Lauder favors were stolen. I chaired a ballet benefit, and one of the guests stole my seat—the one I had reserved for myself, closest to Baryshnikov. Once I was seated next to a picture-book handsome man at a *National Review* anniversary party. Women who hadn't bothered to speak to me for years now stood in line to greet me. I was quite pleased and flattered. I was told later that the man on my right was called Tom Selleck.

It was fun at times, the synthetic glamour; it was also stressful and ultimately empty. I had felt a small sense of accomplishment only during the two years I worked at Bill's magazine, *National Review*. I had never been trained for a profession, never expected to work. It was my sister Priscilla's idea. How I jumped at the chance to prove myself. Ray seemed happy to let me have this time and was patient and supportive of my first tremulous attempts at writing.

I liked the ebb and flow of magazine work, the flurry and pressure before going to press, the short period of containment and calm after. We, the junior editors, spoiled by our managing editor, my sister Priscilla, snuck long lunches then, hiding from Bill Rusher, our publisher. Bill Rusher does not ebb and flow. During the end-of-the-week quiet days, we attended to manuscripts and answered letters to the editor. I wrote a comment on a history professor's article and, by mistake, enclosed and returned it with the manuscript: "Trite—the poor man can't write!"

Bill, my brother and the editor-in-chief, spent each February in Switzerland writing his Blackford Oates novels. For some reason, we hatched a joke on him and wrote an entire phony "The Week" section in as cloying and tasteless prose as we could muster. I wrote the following paragraph about the Chilean coup:

> When the left-coalition government of Marxist president Salvador Allende y Gossens was toppled by a rightist coup engineered by Army General Augusto Pinochet Ugarte . . . hope glimmered that Chile would soon return to normalcy. It's taking, as they say in Spain, some *tiempo*!
>
> Seems too, some of those National Stadium stories are true. Granted the generals are having a hard row to hoe making the MAPUistas toe the line, but let's put soccer back where it belongs and Chile back where *it* belongs. As the Incas said of yore, "The best path is the middle of the road!"

One editor's paragraph ended: "*Quod licet Jovus non licent boves*, as Bill Buckley likes to say." Another's made mention of Justice Douglas's "motorized old ticker," and a third, to Senator Bill ("let it grow") Proxmire. We laughed and laughed, and ran from office to office, reading aloud our contributions, trading advice on how to make them even worse, more offensive, more appalling.

We inserted the section so cleverly into Bill's copy of the magazine—the Swiss Edition, we called it—that he was fooled and accepted it as real. Bill was devastated, and telexed a distraught memo to Priscilla beginning, "I was terribly distressed on reading the editorial paragraphs in the current issue. . . . The paragraphs, or a lot of them, are truly appalling." Of my Chilean paragraph, he commented, "The seizure of coyness in this section is quite impossible to understand. . . . It makes me weep."

191

I left NR after two delightful years because I couldn't handle my life—the two homes, the trips, and our six children. I wonder, if I hadn't left the magazine, if things might have been different; I might have become less dependent on Ray's approval of me and he, in turn, might have found me more interesting. Instead, I continued my role as hostess-wife-mommy, a pampered one to be sure. I had passed Go, won the lottery, and bought Park Place. I talked on the phone, I had lunches at Mortimer's, I raced to M. Marc for hair highlighting and French manicures and to Bloomingdale's for clothes I didn't need, I gave more parties. And all this while there was a real life going on, my children moving into adolescence and young adulthood; Tommy and Buck were at Yale and Emory, Dawn at Bennington, and Anne at Ethel Walker's. Only Carol and Serge were still in New York, Carol finishing up at the Convent of the Sacred Heart, Serge at Buckley School. My husband was also moving into other worlds. It was the beginning of the affluent eighties, and the show of money was nowhere more apparent than in the world of art and of art collecting.

The Burchfields were put away, and the seventeenth-century drawings. The new rage, neo-Expressionist Anselm Kiefer, was collected and erected, and the apartment began to look as homey as a Holocaust museum. Wrapped crates arrived at our apartment and at the house in the country. Some would never be unpacked, some went to storage. My husband bought more and more art and spent more and more time in SoHo—where it was *at*. The art was voguish now, no longer a visual experience. Art now *said* something; like graffiti, it had become political and linear, even politically correct, and on the whole, self-serving and depressing. Somehow, a satiric David Salle slipped onto our bedroom wall—a Mickey Mouse leering at a nude female.

If someone else had slipped into my bedroom, I wouldn't have known, couldn't have borne to know—I needed my innocence still, needed to believe that Ray and I loved each other and that we could stay together.

I was busy, and drinking, not drinking more, but drinking more seriously, my relationship with alcohol growing more dependent and more intimate. I began to feel removed, mechanical, as though I marched to someone else's tune. I did—it was what I knew, what I had always done. I didn't know there was another way, and if I had, I would have been too frightened to explore it. I didn't know that I could make it on my own, that I had the courage and ability to fend for myself. And so, like a little mouse on a treadmill, I raced and raced to make Ray happy, to make the children happy, to please friends and relatives, panting, breathless, at times, exhausted. And as is always the case when you repress and repress, a creative part of me remained locked away, languishing and empty. I was finding it difficult to be there in any real and meaningful sense for others, and least of all for myself. But then, of course, I hadn't yet learned who myself was.

It came between Ray and me, the drinking. And the money and what money breeds. I must have disappointed him. But when finally I stopped drinking, I stopped trying to be the woman he wanted me to be, the person I wasn't. And so the marriage died. For now I bored him. He told me so.

 *Twenty-four*

*I*t is an August evening in our house in Sharon, a beautiful eighteenth-century farmhouse on a green hill overlooking a little valley. A stream runs through it—the children call it Treasure Island. The boys fish there, especially when it is newly stocked with baby trout (they throw them back, or so they promise); the girls play make-believe or adventure. Sometimes they push each other into the stream and come in muddy and cross. I am alone this evening with only Anne and Carol. I don't know why, or where Tommy is, or Buck. Ray is in town, there is an important opening at an important gallery, and my stepchildren, Dawn and Serge, are with their mother in Montauk. Maybe the girls and I are in Sharon to enjoy one last summer week together? I feel a sadness at losing my children, as if they'd gone before I really had time to know them. The time has flown. How frivolously I seem to have spent it!

I pour myself a Scotch and walk into the kitchen to make hot dogs for supper. I don't know why we are eating so early, and in the kitchen, only that I feel too tired to start

194

*up the grill outside. I am very tired these days. I pour
another Scotch.*

*Anne and Carol run upstairs after dinner to watch
television. I move into our library to finish whatever novel
I am reading. I pour a little cognac into a balloon glass. An
after-dinner drink for after dinner. It is six-fifteen.*

*It must have been a good novel, or an engrossing one
at least, because now it is nine-thirty and I am feeling
parched and thirsty—brandy will do that to you. I kiss the
girls good night and return to the kitchen for a little grapefruit juice, grapefruit juice in a tall glass with vodka. Re-
freshing . . .*

*As I pour my second grapefruit juice and vodka—or is
it the third?—the half-gallon bottle slips, and vodka spills
onto the bar. I lean down and lick it up. With my tongue.
I am much too sleepy to keep reading down here. I'll read
in bed . . . and finish my drink.*

*Somehow I cannot navigate the steps. I lurch, my
dressing gown hem is in the way, my feet are caught up in
it. I think how to do this—how to master the stairs. Pick
up dressing gown in one hand, the book hand. Leave the
drink hand free. No, no, that doesn't work. I'm tripping
again, weaving from side to side.*

*Ahh . . . now I see! Place the drink above you, two or
three steps up, then crawl. Crawl—that is how to get upstairs. Now pick up the drink again. Put it down as far as
your arm can reach. Now crawl to it. Good, good . . . I am
almost there. Almost to the bed.*

*I get under the covers—too tired to brush my teeth
and wash. I drink some more vodka-juice. When I pick up
the book, I find that something has happened so that the
type is blurred. I cannot see it anymore. Might as well take
another little drink and turn off the light.*

Oh, God—it is then that the room begins to move, rocking, swaying—I am nauseated; saliva streams down the back of my throat. I'm afraid that I will throw up, all over myself in bed. I am blind drunk. "Oh, God," I moan out loud. "You are an alcoholic, you are an alcoholic. . . ." The black sets in.

I woke up sick with terror, hung over, and shaky. I had gotten that drunk, on a peaceful summer evening, in my pretty summer house, by myself. Drinking all by myself. That is one of "the signs." You see, I hadn't avoided reading about alcoholism; I was aware of my love affair with alcohol. In fact, I understood that there would come a time when we must part. I knew that that's how it's done, nothing so simple, or impossible, as cutting down. You have to quit. I'd read enough to know that.

But . . . I didn't have blackouts, those fleeting periods of amnesia described in the literature. I didn't drink in the morning. I didn't sneak drinks. I'd never gotten into trouble with my drinking (unless, of course, you examined my entire adult life); no one had ever mentioned my drinking . . . except my stepdaughter, Dawn, but then it was only that one time aboard the *France*. Besides, Dawn didn't like me much.

They call these "the yets": and yet I haven't been arrested for drunk driving; and yet I haven't had the DTs; and yet . . .

I stopped drinking three weeks later in New York City. I had help, lots of help, hands that reached out to me and held me up, fellow travelers who encouraged me, listened with patience to my piteous plaints, endured my mood swings. The Swiss analyst Carl Jung, in correspondence with Bill Wilson, the founder of Alcoholics Anonymous, said that alcoholics cannot be "cured" without undergoing a spiritual experience. Maybe, for stopping drinking is a very hard thing to do, and during the early weeks and months, learning to live another way, to live sober, is akin to having all seven layers of your skin peeled off. I seemed to have no defenses, no tolerance, no self-understanding, and no true knowledge of the world around me. It had always been coated sticky with booze, my feelings tamped down with it, my anxieties subdued.

I am wearing a summer evening dress, bare-backed, and I shiver in the frigid air—recycled, air-conditioned suburban air. I am at the home of a business associate of my husband's. It smells of stale smoke. It is nine o'clock, and around me the guests are talking louder, laughing louder, patting, punching arms, repeating themselves—louder and louder. I know only a few persons here, my host and hostess, some business friends, my husband. I am lost in this crowd, dwarfed behind slender tanned backs, behind tall men with no socks and bright linen jackets, behind uniformed waitresses, bartenders, trays of liquor I do not drink. Do-not-drink, do-not-drink, do-not-drink.

I feel the tension in my neck and shoulders from straining to look up at people, five feet of me struggling to respond to what I can't hear them saying; I feel the dryness in my throat from trying to raise my voice to be heard, but as the strangers I speak to are yelling too, it doesn't really matter, for no one even pretends to listen. The maid passes another tired platter of hors d'oeuvres, wilted and curling at the edges. Eat it, whatever it is. Do-not-drink, do-not-drink . . .

Crabmeat, crabmeat in a dust-dry puff.

"So nice to see you too . . ."

The music begins, too bouncy and loud. A hand takes my shoulder. It is my husband asking me to dance. He looks over my head at all the important people, the people he should be talking to, the people I am meant to be talking to. The people we are here to see and be seen by.

"Are they ever going to serve dinner?" I ask.

"For God's sake, we just got here. Loosen up, why don't you?"

More talk-talk, lines to stand in, buffets to eat, strangers to sit by, talk to make. Dance, dance, talk. Talk. No one hears. Do-not-drink. Do-not-drink.

No one hears.

It is a quarter of one in the morning. He has asked me to dance again.

"Can't we go now?"

"What's wrong with you? People are having a good time. Have a glass of champagne. One glass of champagne won't hurt you."

Do-not-drink. Do-not-drink. Spoilsport. Wet blanket. Party-poop. Bore . . .

I felt a nakedness as I was becoming sober. There was nothing left to shield and protect me from the outside world and from other people. Even my body seemed to change, to come alive, as if from a deep sedated sleep. In the first months of sobriety I felt the air and the sunlight in a different and more vivid way, I felt the flow and heat of them like a baby, and reveled in the experience with the same wonderment and glee. For there are as many mysterious and exciting times becoming sober as there are stressful and confusing ones.

The weight of "feeling" began to separate into quite discrete emotions. I no longer felt "good" or "bad." I felt loving, amused, affectionate, proud, lighthearted, angry, jealous, absorbed, bored, shamed, enthralled, appreciated. It was like having a gray light explode into the colors of the rainbow. What had been dulled by the drug now became vivid and acute. Becoming sober is an exhausting experience because it is so intense, so *real*.

It was reality that I had to accept. No more champagne, no more bubbles, no more fantasy. My brain stopped playing tricks, my memory sharpened, and my attention intensified. The people I used to know felt uncomfortable around me; the people I got to know made me laugh, and sometimes cry. I had been a prisoner of privilege for many years, locked away from the world. Now, in the course of my recovery, I met a prostitute who had become a psychologist, I met a nun who had become a social worker—and married and had twins. I went sailing one afternoon with an editor from the *New York Times,* a television soap actress, a graduate of Sing Sing and Dannemora, and a jazz musician. And they all knew more about life and the living of it than I. I listened.

Another part of the sobering-up process took longer and felt more like work. For in letting go of my delusions, I had to begin the journey through self-deception and become honest, with myself and with others. Neither I, nor others, particularly appreciated this. There were shifts in old friendships and shifts in my being, for there was no place left to hide, no amber liquid to hide in. I began to understand aspects of myself, to *recognize* them. Among the things I learned is that I have always relished quiet, the familiar, familial quiet of my childhood bedroom. I learned that I have an aversion to noise, to crowds. I learned that I have a big heart and empathy for the hurt and the lonely and the hopeless, for I have been all three. I learned that I was tired of working so very hard for love, and I learned that I had a hunger to learn. This process took time, months and years.

I had married Tom without finishing college. And so I began my junior year of college in 1982. I was forty-three years old. That fall, in the midst of midterms, I came to understand that I had become an intrusion on Ray's new lifestyle. The eyes that had once delighted in me now looked at me with dislike. I once heard a woman say, "I fell madly in love with him—and so did he." As I began to take my first faltering steps away from Ray's heady embrace, began to develop interests and opinions of my own, and friends, the glass cracked. I was no longer the mirror of his own perfect image.

I carried his rejection of me like a rock. I cried for no reason, walking down the street, riding on the bus, sitting in class. I cried when we met at restaurants, at movie theaters. I cried in the morning when he left for work. If you had asked me, I could not have told you why. If you had asked me if the marriage was over, I would have denied it.

The final outburst came one evening at an election-night party for Lew Lehrman, who was running for governor. My husband arrived late and intoxicated, angry to have been taken away from whomever he had been with. I asked him to make room at the ballroom railing and, enraged, he screamed: "Why don't you get the fuck out of my life!"

The friends who had brought me, took me home. They were shocked and careful with me; my friend Mary offered to stay the night.

We managed to get through a pretend Thanksgiving and pretend Christmas holidays. After the children returned to school, we flew to Barbados. I remember it as my idea. I thought we might come together there, away from

the divisive distractions of the city. On the plane, Ray became so agitated that he paced the aisle, back and forth.
Once there, on the beautiful white beaches, in our beautiful
resort hotel, well, there was nothing to say, words I had
rehearsed stayed unspoken in futility and fear. In the past
there had never been enough words for the two of us. We
came together in torrents of words and love; we sneaked
out of parties to be alone together, preferred each other's
company to anyone else's. For despite his possessive outbursts, despite my own passive retreats, we had talked and
trusted and shared each other.

Now there were terrible silences, a frightening listless-
ness and apathy in the daylight, and at night, when he
slept, I opened the sliding glass doors of our room and
walked the beach, my breath coming in gasps, my heart
flapping like a caged animal. It was a terrible, awkward
trip, a terrible idea to imagine that we could bridge the
relentless chasm between us with swaying palms and soft
nights.

On the day after our return, I remember feeling a brief
moment of release, of happiness almost. My mother's medical reports showed that she did not have the cancer we had
suspected and feared. Ray and I dined at a neighborhood
restaurant that evening with Serge. We were laughing,
Serge and I, joking together. All of a sudden, his father
flared with anger: I had not, it seemed, paid adequate attention to something he had said. I remember the feeling of
being punched, all happiness and lighthearted banter
knocked out of me. We finished supper in silence, Serge's
eyes glued to the table. Walking up Third Avenue, Ray and
Serge strode ahead, leaving me to follow behind.

I knew—it happened just like that, on a cold January
evening walking north on Third near Seventy-third, the

clear understanding that it was finished. I would not continue to live this way. I followed Ray into the library and said, "I have to leave. I can't live this way anymore."

He asked me to stay; he proposed that we maintain two apartments, one downtown that he could stay in "when he felt like it"—an extra apartment for him and his "art" friends. He was surprised that I found this unreasonable, untenable—surprised and perhaps amused, too, because the joke was on me. He already had the second apartment.

He looked sad, he looked depressed, he complained that he was broke, and so, being in what I remember as the "spiritual" phase of my recovery from alcoholism, I found a spiritual lawyer and filed for a proper spiritual divorce—no money, no paintings, no property. I wanted Ray to know that I wasn't about money, that love and money are very separate things. In March of 1983, with all my children now away at college, I moved to a rental apartment at Eighty-third and Third. I moved in with Calvin, a six-month-old Maltese puppy.

Twenty-five

Calvin and I stayed that summer in Manhattan. I walked him in the park on weekends, took summer courses, and began learning to be alone. I discovered coffee shops and Sunday breakfasts with the *Times*. I learned to go to movies by myself and to concerts. I never have quite learned to go to big parties, though, and so I seldom do. And I learned to make my own friends. It had never occurred to me that I must take the initiative, that I must telephone, that I must make the date for lunch, that I must arrange to have people in for supper. I had a single friend, Mimi, and she told me about that.

Mimi wears a hat. On Mimi, hats fit, just so, appropriate and smart. We sit at an overpriced fish restaurant on Third Avenue. I have been talking nonstop, and I'm aware of the frantic undertone in my voice. Despite the thoughtful attention Mimi has given me throughout, I know I have been boring. I speak only of Ray these days. Ray, Ray, Ray—his specter haunts my mind and heart and conversation. For I have left and not left him, not made the final separation

*from him to me. I don't know who I am without him.
About my own fears, my uncertainties, and the lostness
that I feel when I am alone, I have no words.*

*My friend nods her head in sympathy and, searching
my face, asks, "Have I ever told you what it was like to be
an unmarried woman in the fifties and sixties?"*

No.

*Had I ever asked? Ever thought to ask, for always
since knowing Mimi I had been smugly and contentedly
married.*

"Tell me."

*"Well, it was very difficult. A bad time. Friend after
friend got married, paired off, began families, and I . . . I
was what they called a career girl. That meant working for
a living. I didn't work for a living because I was emanci-
pated—I worked because I needed to, because there was
no one else to pay the bills.*

*"Now when I went to parties I went alone. Even
when I had a date, I felt alone because everyone there
was a married couple and my friends' concerns were now
about their children, schools, summer camps. I, on the
other hand, had more in common with their husbands,
with business, earning a living. But there I was the odd
man out as well. There weren't many of us professional
women, you see, so men weren't comfortable talking to
us."*

*She looks across the table at me in her kind, direct
way, telling me for the first time about herself, about ex-
periencing a time when single women were called old
maids, spinsters.*

*"Oh, Mimi, I never thought—the thought of going
out alone, I don't know how to do it. I never thought how
it must have been for you."*

204

I hadn't, hadn't even thought to ask my own unmar-
ried sister Priscilla, hadn't had the curiosity to wonder.

"Well, dear, you'll be just fine. It takes getting used to.
It takes making the effort. If you want to see people, you'll
have to be the one to do the phoning and asking."

She smiles, encouraging me, and raises her glass of
white wine as if to toast me, to wish me well on the journey
ahead.

I managed the college part easily, still waking in tears,
still dreaming nightly about my husband, surprised at
dawn to find myself alone. I threw myself into my studies,
became a psych major, and at the same time took the five
required courses mandated by the state of New York to
become an alcoholism counselor. But the most difficult
thing was to learn to think of myself as "I" instead of
"we," for I was suddenly without a role, without an identity, and "student" didn't qualify.

My son Tommy was finishing at Yale, Buck was at Emory, Anne abroad for her junior year, and Carol starting the
University of Virginia. I was not a wife, just a part-time
mother of grown children, not a daughter—a who? After
managing two households of from two to six children and
attending to the needs of my husband, I now lived in a small
apartment with a small dog. I also had to begin, resistantly,
to look at my finances. I had been responsible for my children's tuition, and now I had my own tuition to pay as well.
I had never learned to negotiate for money, to ask for it, and
so when Tom asked that he no longer be responsible for the
children's tuition, I finally agreed. When, after our marriage, Ray and I continued to use our own separate bank
accounts for household expenses, well, I thought that was
only fair. My marriages were quite costly.

Single once more, the author with nephew Christopher Buckley at Patricia's sixtieth birthday party.

In a most typical Buckley fashion, my brother Bill helped me out. I had spoken to Reid over the phone, and we indulged in our monthly groan about money. Now it happened that Reid told Bill and then that Bill called Priscilla, wondering if it would offend me to receive help. Priscilla telephoned me. It took me some days to think about it—I was aware of my own extravagances and felt guilty. I was not spending Cartier kinds of money, but always, always spending just a little more than I had. Then, without Bill ever having spoken to me, a monthly check began to arrive at the bank. It would see me through my graduate degree at NYU and afford me my last years in New York.

I was lonely those last years in New York, still hoping for someone to care for me and to take care of me. Taking care of yourself is a difficult thing to learn in middle age. So is feeling expendable. So is being alone. I remember that one of the hardest times was to return from a trip and have no one expecting me, no one to know whether I had arrived safely or not, no one to have missed me. My friend Ellie understood this better than I, and she kept track of my comings and goings and called, left me messages, welcomed me home. I was learning to rely on these women, on Ellie and Betsey and Joan and Claudia and Rose—my phalanx of strong women friends.

Yet though they were there for me, they could not be there with me, in the bedroom when I woke up, in the late afternoon when I came in tired from school. Not when the seasons changed. That is a difficult time to be on your own, the change of seasons, especially watching the first snow. It is always wondrous, the new snow, the white silence of it blanketing the earth. "Oh, look, it's snowing!" I want to say.

A sense of my own autonomy would develop slowly as I learned to focus on others and to leave myself behind. In the fall of 1985, just before graduating from Marymount, I began an internship at Freedom Institute as part of my substance-abuse training. It was not your garden variety alcohol recovery center: it was situated in a town house at Madison and Seventy-fourth, and our clients were Social Register—Fifth Avenue matrons, Wall Street lawyers, and even a movie star sprinkled here and there.

Mona Mansell had founded Freedom Institute as the first intervention center on the East Coast. Connie Murray directed the interventions with such skill that numbers of the newly sober-intervened returned to Manhattan from rehabilitation wanting more therapy—what we in the business call "aftercare." The center offered group and individual counseling. It was in that end that I worked and learned. I was scared and anxious—I anticipated provoking drunken relapses, divorces, suicides. I anticipated flunking Therapist 101.

I led a women's recovery group and had a female group member develop a Scope addiction as she proceeded to waft out of group on waves of intoxicating peppermint. Beware the "recovering" alcoholic who smells of mouthwash! I sent an English lord to treatment and sobered up the founder of a fist club. I sometimes joked about the work, covered over the intensity of it with laughter, but I saw the saddest people I had ever seen and heard the saddest tales I had ever heard. I saw families broken apart, despondent parents, depressed adolescents.

I co-facilitated groups, I did intakes, made assessments, referrals, wrote treatment plans, and held individual counseling sessions. I had a two-hundred-pound man fall drunk on my lap—after telling me he hadn't had a drink in months.

"Oh, my," I say, "you haven't had a drink for how long?"

My client has gotten himself up from the floor to his knees. Holding on to my desk with both hands, and reeking of liquor, he smiles up at me with a silly, ingratiating grin.

"Titinitious . . . titinitus."

"Titinitious?" I repeat. Should I call someone? Will he fall again? Will he pass out? Die?

"That's why I fell. Inner ear, you know . . ." He lurches to the door of my office and, leaning against the jamb, waves. "A bad case of titinitus. Bye-bye, shee you . . ."

"Oh . . ."

All that schooling just to learn to say "Oh." But at least it is an empathic "oh," a definite mirroring kind of "oh."

Now what?

They don't teach you how to handle the now-whats? in school. Textbooks don't have now-what? cases in them. Other, more experienced therapists would do that for me, and some, like my friend and colleague Claudia, led me by the hand, supported and encouraged me, allowing me to learn from my mishaps.

What we shared at Freedom Institute was a deeply held belief that our clients could get better. We were an eclectic clinical staff: an ex-cop, whose psychodrama groups resounded through the thin walls, an Episcopalian monk, alcohol counselors, social workers, behaviorists, and the earnest overanalyzed. And despite our different backgrounds and clinical perspectives, many of our clients actually moved, or were "eased," into recovery, repairing their shattered lives and starting anew.

One of the male counselors and I ran a group of mostly men. We had a publisher, a former stockbroker now working as a cabdriver, a real estate entrepreneur, the owner of a chain of Irish bars, and an actor. They would constitute the final group because one by one the female members were either pushed out or jumped ship. Women were alternately mocked, condescended to, or simply ignored. I was the only woman the men couldn't banish; I was their counselor and they were stuck with me.

The group focused on position and power, a hierarchical meeting of middle-aged males, hell-bent on keeping up the walls—a mighty compound of male chauvinists. They boasted about their golf scores, their salaries, their girlfriends, especially the married ones—this very probably for my benefit, their virgin therapist (more like a virgin sacrifice)—and any attempts I made to bring feelings into the room were thwarted. Of their alcoholism and of the ruin it had brought them, they chose not to speak. If I

AT THE STILL POINT

mentioned it, if I wondered aloud why we were meeting at an alcoholism facility on this weekly basis, they simply changed the subject or spoke over me. Or, sometimes, they flirted and coyly answered the "little woman."

"You know so much, Carol, you tell us!"

One evening, as a member described a visit to his dying aunt, his voice broke. Usually he played the role of group clown, deflecting all feeling with wit. I saw an opening and jumped in feet first. "You seem sad as you describe this, are you . . ."

The man sitting next to me sucked in his breath and in a deadly monotone began mouthing: "Cunt, whore, fucking dyke—you fucking Geraldine Ferraro"—I had Ferraro-streaked hair, cut short that summer—"bitch, fucking stinking bitch-whore lesbian shit . . ." My attacker continued foully, scraping his chair up to mine, his face suffused with red.

I looked for help. There was no one to rescue me. The other men in the group were as shocked as I, as frightened. I held my hands together to keep them from shaking. I felt my own cheeks blazing hot, but I did not change my expression. I continued to face him, absorbing his inchoate rage, and said, "Yes, yes . . . yes, yes . . ." in as soothing a voice as I could summon. He ran out of obscenities at last, ran down like a choking, sputtering engine and, putting his face in his hands, he stood abruptly, knocking over his chair, and fled the room. The psychotherapist, I was discovering, must combine sensitivity with nerves of steel.

Some nights after group, at eight or nine, after a twelve-hour stint of work, I would walk over to Madison to catch the bus uptown. The bus stopped in front of the Whitney Museum.

•

210

My head is pounding. In group, a distraught member has alternately sobbed and berated me. I have role-played her rejecting mother for the last time! I am stiff with fatigue, weighed down by a sodden raincoat, the wilted scarf on my head soaked through. My hair lies in dank strands across my forehead. My shoes are wet, little boats awash with dirty street water—and the idiotic bus won't come! I peer down Madison, through the sheets of rain, and all I see are massed cabs, cars, headlights shimmering through the downpour. And limousines . . .

The Whitney is having an opening. Ah, another opening—tonight I think it's Eric Fischl. The museum is ablaze with lights, patrons in black tie and flounced Gaultier evening dresses scurry through the great glass doors. Men are posted at the entrance with huge golf umbrellas in bright reds and yellows. Silly, I think, ostentatious—as if the guests couldn't carry their own umbrellas!

I look into the downstairs and see the caterers preparing the dinner tables. They are using Glorious Foods—I recognize the crudité platters and the grapes rolled in chevre. I recall having seen a couple of the waiters before. I spot Tom Armstrong, the museum president, and though I cannot see them from this distance, I wager that he is wearing his fourteen-karat-gold "safety pin" studs.

And Ray . . .

The man hurrying down the street to the entryway is my estranged husband. He flashes his smile at the elegant young woman clinging to his arm. Beneath her cape I spot the bouffant hem of a lipstick-red dress. Above, red lips and shiny, thick black hair.

Poor me, poor little match girl standing in the cold! There were times I yearned to have him back, for I had

211

truly loved him. But I knew that I would never be able to summon the strength to leave again, and I knew that he would not change. When I visualized returning to Ray, I imagined myself climbing back into a life-sized bottle of booze and screwing on the cap. There, trapped inside like a ghostly floating specimen, a nice pickled smiley me.

❀ *Twenty-six*

I visit my mother. My sisters and I have tried to make this New York apartment Mother-like. But it isn't. The life isn't there, the bric-a-brac she fiddles with and moves from place to place, the flowers. We bring flowers, but I'm not sure she cares, or notices. She doesn't really know why she is here—she thinks she's on her way back to Camden.

I have been chosen to accompany her through the Beekman Hotel board procedure, so that the board can "pass" her, allow her to live in the building. Or perhaps I volunteer. It is still very important for me to be acknowledged by my older brothers and sisters and to be useful to them. I am a wreck. My mother is incontinent, and very stubborn about not wearing her pads; she sees nothing, but continues to pretend that she can, and she is given to saying outrageous things. "I never did like her," she said to my nephew about his dead mother. Just recently, she asked her own sister Inez, "And how is your dear mother?" Her mother, my grandmother, dead years and years before.

Mother has, however, stopped telling people, all bright

anticipation, that today is the day she is going to die. At least I hope she has. . . .

Will she wet? Will she knock over the canapés? Will she tell a board member that his ears stick out? Fortunately, the Beekman houses so many geriatric residents that all the stairs have ramps, and the board members are understanding. They are gracious. They ask gentle questions, which I rush to answer for her. My mother smiles benignly.

"And now, Mrs. Buckley, have you any questions for us?"

"No," I interject.

"Yes," she announces. Mother looks about the room and says to nobody in particular, "I'd like to know who you are and what I'm doing here."

What a laugh we all have at that! Mother too—she thinks she's said something awfully clever. I manipulate her toward the door before she decides to stay and have another little cocktail. All these lovely people! Mr. ——— sees us to the door, and my mother turns to him and asks gaily, "Do you know what today is?"

She is seated in a yellow armchair in a yellow room that somehow has aged more mustard than canary. She has fuzzy white hair and vague eyes. She smiles. Mary has helped her dress. Mary has come up from Camden to care for her, and Mary's sister, who lives in Brooklyn, takes the night shift. We have tried hiring white nurses, but Mother resents and resists them. Mary, however, she will obey. Mary she trusts.

My mother is wearing a bright green silk dress and stockings and high-heeled shoes. She has lipstick on and

214

earrings and the Oriental pearls my father gave her for a wedding anniversary. She is picking at a little bowl of cocktail nibbles, salty ones—she is so southern she still puts salt on cantaloupe—and fiddling with a glass of white wine. She has one or two before her supper.

I hurry to speak before Mary can open her mouth to ask me one more time "How come you left that nice Mr. Ray?" My mother doesn't know about my separation; in fact my mother doesn't really know that I am me. Sometimes I am Priscilla, sometimes "dear Jane."

"How are you, Mother? Did you have a nice day?"

"Oh, yes, dear, lovely. I just came, you see, from Venezuela. To visit your father. I went on a boat."

"Oh, that's wonderful. I hope you're not tired from the trip."

"Me, tired? I'm never tired. You see, I'm going to Camden tomorrow. Aloise is coming with me, and the children."

"My goodness—all her children! It will be a busy train ride."

"No, silly we're flying on . . . that thing . . . the thing that whirrrrrs . . ."

"The plane . . ."

She is silent now, too confused momentarily to try to go on. A great sadness clouds her face, she reaches for my hand, then holds on to my wrist with very cool, soft fingers. She grasps it tight. "I am so worried," she says, "I am so worried about my baby. . . ."

Of course! She has worried about me, worried through my depression, my failed marriage, my loss of faith. Of course, she has known and cared. I take her hand, holding back my tears for all the years that she has loved me and never said so.

Oh, no, Mother, please, no . . . Don't break my heart, don't worry about me anymore.

She cannot hear my words, for, like her, I do not speak them aloud.

My mother would die two years later on March 10, 1985, the eve of her ninetieth birthday, after a month spent in silence in the Sharon Hospital. Her sister Inez has died; my brother John has died. When John died on the first of December, he was buried beside his wife, Ann, in Salisbury. My mother's nursing home, where we were finally forced to place her last year, was near the cemetery. Just before the service, my friend Marvin Liebman and I decided to run over and visit with her for a moment. Mother hadn't been told of John's death.

She was nowhere to be found, not in her bedroom, not in her sitting room, not in the common room. Finally a floor nurse told us, "Mrs. Buckley asked her nurse to drive her by the cemetery. She said, 'My son is being buried there today, but I don't want anyone to know that I know.' "

And so there wasn't much to keep my mother here. She missed my father and the children who had gone before her. Sensitive as always, she took the entire month to expire, giving all her loved ones the chance to visit and to say good-bye. My son Tommy came, and Anne.

The children sit on either side of her, holding her hands. They are gentle with her, accepting of her silence. I begin to sing one of Mother's old songs, "Pat O'Shea." She taps her foot in time—otherwise, she neither moves nor speaks. There is nothing left for us to say.

Twenty-seven

Now, having made such a smashing success of my own life, I would become a fixer of others'. I studied psychodrama with Jim Sacks down in the Village, and took some workshops on Gestalt, perfecting conversations with empty chairs. I participated in week-long seminars on experiential group therapy and learned aspects of family therapy at the Ackerman Institute. I attended lectures on psychoanalysis ("The Case of the Man with the Imagined Vulva") and on Kohut's "self psychology." I heard a feisty, cynical Albert Ellis speak, and also R. D. Laing. He poked fun at us, at our pretensions of mental health and diagnostic flim-flam (he didn't act schizophrenic one bit). I took the Road Less Traveled with Dr. Scott Peck. I came to earth with a thud and began a graduate program in clinical social work at NYU in 1987. My friends Joan and Claudia had preceded me there; Joan and Claudia had warned me that social work will do that to you, bring you thudding down to earth.

Studying psychological theorists is a fascinating discipline, a mind game, embroidered with as much myth and fable as fact. Studying social work, on the other hand, is to come face to face with human misery. Nothing dramatic or romantic here, only want and deprivation and the absolute understanding that life is not just. Other graduate schools display posters of Crete and Sardinia, Guns N' Roses, Cindy Crawford, David Letterman; schools of social work display pictures of battered women, patients in the end stages of AIDS, and hollow-faced children with emaciated limbs and swollen stomachs.

I had now moved to First and Ninety-third. I bought a West Highland white terrier puppy, Daisy, to cheer me up and to keep Calvin company during my long hours away at NYU. Daisy ate up the entire apartment twice, parquet flooring, rugs, sofa pillows, and ottoman. I called in a trainer, Bash Dibra, and the dogs cowered instantly and be-haved in his presence. In between our sessions, I seldom did what he had asked me to. Ten minutes before his appointed time, I would rush the dogs through their commands: "Sit! Stay! Stop!" Bash terminated me as untrainable.

It was through my scrappy dogs that I met Doc. My Maltese, Calvin, who weighs eleven pounds, has an in-flated self-image. His penchant for attacking pit bulls and shepherds had already landed him in surgery twice. I began sneaking out of the building with the dogs in the early morning hours, using the freight elevator to avoid conflict with the big-dog owners. Doc worked as a porter and building guard. He sat at a small table smoking, and while he was somewhat taciturn with me, he loved the dogs, especially the voracious Daisy, whom he called his honey: "How's my honey? How's Doc's li'l honey today?"

Daisy, sated after a night's down-pillow marauding, would wiggle her rear end and place her head on Doc's lap, all sweetness and affection. One morning after Doc had returned from vacation, he told me he'd been "down home."

"Where's home, Doc?" I had caught some lyrical *r*'s underlying his New York speech.

"Greenville, South Carolina."

"Oh, my," I said, "I was brought up in Camden."

There was a moment's pause as Doc digested this new piece of information. After thinking it over, he looked at me and smiled. "I bet your house was bigger than mine," he said.

From then on, we chatted regularly. One morning, looking bashful, he told me, "Last night, I got inducted into the Rock and Roll Hall of Fame."

I stared at him, taking in his broad, handsome face, his familiar face. Nothing clicked. Nothing came to mind, and I was left with a feeble "Oh?"

"I'm one of the Drifters. One of the original ones."

So Doc was Doc Green, one of the four Drifters, black kids who began singing on the streets of Harlem and went on to make the gold records I had danced to as a teenager. Billy Joel, presenting the award, cited "Up on the Roof" as the song that had inspired him to begin composing. I remembered the Drifters well, their rhythm and humor and optimism. I remembered Doc's vibrant voice.

He looked up at me. "You're wondering how come I'm here?"

It wasn't that unusual, his story of drunkenness and lost times, but the ending was special: "I ended up in Chicago on a gig, so sick I thought I'd die. I wanted to die. My wife come all the way out by train and brought me home one more time. Took me in one more time."

"What made you stop, Doc? Did you go to AA? Did you have counseling?"

"No, ma'am. I stopped because of the love of a good woman."

Doc took sick. Some months later he came back, wasted and gray, his belt tied around his waist to hold up his trousers, his wrists as fragile as a child's. "How's my honey?" he whispered. I brought Calvin and Daisy down to visit, but I could see they tired him. I kissed him and took the dogs back upstairs. I had purchased a 1950's album with "Save the Last Dance for Me." I played it in the car and listened for Doc's strong baritone. Returning to the city a few weeks later, just after Christmas, the tape snapped, and when I pulled it out, it was twisted beyond repair. That night Ray Gomez, our doorman, rang the bell of my apartment. "I knew you'd want to know that Doc died this morning."

As part of my NYU training, I worked at a second internship at a center for the elderly poor. I visited the aged and the mentally ill in their apartments. These clients had no anger left, only a mute acceptance of their deteriorating lives.

One client, Mrs. L., had come from society. Some of the other workers didn't like her because she had highfalutin airs. Maria didn't like her, and Maria handled our most difficult clients, especially our (very few) old men. "No," Maria screamed into the phone one day—in geriatric centers a scream is your normal tone of voice. "No, Mr. ——, you are not to take off your clothes again. No! We are not having surgery today—we're having the dentist. The *dentist*!" Maria lit another Camel Light, "Christ on a crutch," she groaned and then, back into the phone, "Your *bridge*, Mr. ——! Your teeth. . . . Aw, come on, sweetheart, please, *please* don't take off your clothes. It's not nice. . . ."

220

Mrs. L. had had a lobotomy as a young woman, but her social poise remained, and it was only if you listened carefully that you understood there was nobody there. Mrs. L. and her husband had appeared at the center some years before, he in the terminal stages of Parkinson's disease. When he died, the social workers sent a cleaning crew to the apartment. They found it overrun with cockroaches, and a garbage truck was filled with the detritus of their sad lives: sewage, rotting food, stained bedclothes and carpets. "But the worst," confided Mrs. L. one afternoon, "was when the Yale club posted our name for nonpayment of dues."

"My dear Miss Buckley, how kind of you to visit."

She has been waiting for me, sitting straight in her best chair, some days a tiny brooch, some days a soiled silk flower pinned haphazardly to her breast, sad little reminders that she has primped for the occasion.

"Tea? Do you prefer India or China, Miss Buckley?" Mrs. L. peers across the fusty living room to where her unhappy Medicaid-provided attendant, Betty, is sitting out my visit, and yells in a ratchety, commanding voice: "Betty, Betty—tea for our visitor!"

"Nope."

"Nope? Nope?" Mrs. L. looks at me and shakes her head as if to say, Really, help isn't what it used to be, is it?

"Now, where were we, Miss Buckley? Ah, yes . . . the Yale Club."

"Perhaps I can ask you a few questions first, Mrs. L.?" I am here to discover whether the visiting nurse has checked her insulin level, whether she has taken a walk this week as she promised she would, whether Betty was or was

not at work on Monday when the telephone went unanswered on four separate occasions.

"The Yale Club." Mrs. L. smiles. "Did I ask if you wanted tea?"

"Mrs. L. . . ."

"My husband organized a book party for . . . now, could that be your uncle? Or was it the senator? The senator is your . . . ?"

"Tell me about the visiting nurse, Mrs. L. . . . How is your blood pressure? And your diabetes?"

"Such a lovely occasion! My, but Mr. Buckley spoke eloquently. Or was it the senator? You remember, I'm sure you were there. . . ."

Uncanny, Mrs. L., to know on some level the connections we had one to the other, connections I was not free to reveal. She had once had an apartment in my own Park Avenue building; her mother came from New Orleans, and her parents had met in Mexico. More important, we had both had our experiences of mental illness and mental hospitals. Was that what she sensed? Was that what she wanted to communicate and to share with me?

My client, Mrs. C., was confined to her bed, a mattress on the floor, and refused any help except for a sullen West Indian woman who came in three half-days a week, or didn't come in as the mood struck her. Mrs. C. was ninety-three and frugal. She had a refrigerator on the floor by her bed. She turned on the TV at the foot of the bed with a long stick. On the bed she had her stuffed animals and crocheting materials. She also had a plastic bucket on the floor into which she evacuated. It was emptied every other day, *if* the Jamaican lady made her rounds. If not . . .

I felt faint the first day and carried her stench on my clothes for the rest of the afternoon. As I sat by her bed, cockroaches had scampered up and down my legs. It would take me more than a month to "counsel" her into letting me place traps around the floor. Chubby Mrs. C. lived on ice cream and saltines. She was spending her last years in abysmal circumstances, and yet she stubbornly held on to the reins and retained her autonomy. She was the happiest of all my clients, engaging, humorous, and though I would never mount the stairs without a gag reflex, I came to love and to respect her and to relish her conversation.

She regaled me with stories about her youth. She was Czech, and her uncles and aunts had been button makers by profession and had emigrated to New York to work in the warehouses that lined First Avenue. She knew Manhattan from its trolley days, and once a dwarf chased her home from the circus and tried to seduce her.

She laughed and laughed. "Oh, his funny little legs kicking up and down!"

Her son had died in the adjoining room and for three days she didn't know. They'd had a dog, Ruffie. Before he was taken away from her, Ruffie had come to her bed and put his nose to her neck, as if to say, "We lost our pal, we lost our good pal." I became her good pal, too, and worried throughout the winter, knowing that I would disappear from her life as well. For that is how it is with social work placements: you come for a year and then you disappear and move on to another agency and more learning. But the old are used to losing and it was I who had to fight the tears when I said good-bye. On that last day, breaking all professional conventions, I brought my puppy, Calvin, to play with her.

And then there was Miss K., who threatened to throw herself out of the window and had to be physically removed by the NYPD. I spent hours with her in the psych ward at Metropolitan Hospital. One day, her bed was empty. The nurse told me that they had taken her down to X-Ray. I found her there, all eighty pounds of her, in hysteric convulsions. A hospital porter and a powerfully built technician labored to stretch her body straight, and I saw that they were attempting to bind her legs and arms. I rapped on the glass aperture. "Please," I cried, "please let me in!" I felt her panic, felt my heartbeat accelerate and my breathing begin to speed up.

I was permitted to wear a lead apron and to hold Miss K. during the procedure. She moaned and lamented, but her body relaxed and the spasms abated. I stroked her, speaking low, murmuring over and over, "It's all right; it's going to be all right. . . ." Slowly she quieted, still holding tight to my hand, still needing to be touched. A young Hispanic with a beaten face and needle marks up his arms sat in a wheelchair waiting for X-Ray. As I began to roll Miss K. toward the elevator, he flipped the wheels of his chair and sped forward to intercept us. I was startled, as he had been staring at us throughout. He reached out to touch my arm. "Hey, miss," he said, "I just wanted to say— you're a beautiful lady!"

And so there are rewards to social work. Not the textbook cases in which clients instantly internalize the interventions you make and then live happily after, but small moments when you are there because no one else is, small gifts you tender, tedious little chores like straightening out a Medicaid mishap, placating a landlord. Sometimes you contact a family member, serve as an advocate with Con Ed, alert physicians. You observe, listen, care, offering simple tokens of interest and concern that bring with them, even if just temporarily, a sense of worth and dignity to the recipient.

The pain of being a social worker is that you will leave, be reassigned, often to be replaced by another earnest caretaker and, ultimately, that you will be forgotten. For though I was kind and competent at what I did, I was not irreplaceable. Not one bit. Not ever. And that understanding always comes as quite a blow.

Twenty-eight

During the late eighties in New York, in between the studying and the exams and the case histories and the counseling, I had moments of terrible yearning. I had dated two men, one for two years, one for a year, and they had both moved on to other women. I had loved them just a little, for loving fully entailed the risk of losing myself again. I had, in fact, chosen men who would not bond. That made it safe, and it was also how I thought you dated in the 1980s—the serial, if not quite zipless, affair. Of course it wouldn't work for me, trying to separate sex and love. "Carol," said my friend Dominick, as I moaned over my faithless lovers, "you don't get it, do you? You are *not* a casual fuck."

At the end of each relationship, I agonized, hurt and bewildered. What had I done? Not done? And like the good depressive that I am, I blamed myself. I was middle-aged, I was dumpy, I had lines, I was unlovable and a proven failure at relationships. Once I had had confidence with men; now my attraction for them and my trust in

226

them had waned. I mourned that, felt the loss acutely, found it hard to face the prospect of a life spent single and alone.

New York City was changing for me as well. The streets and neighborhoods that had once teemed with energetic couples, families, young singles emanating well-being and ambition, now felt overcrowded and dingy. People's faces seemed closed and withdrawn, and everywhere the beggars, the drifting homeless and aggressive, dead-eyed addicts. There had been a time when I drew my energy and spirit from the city streets; now they sapped me. I found myself drawn to the country, to the sweet quiet there.

One winter weekend I drove the road from the neighboring town of Lakeville to Sharon. On these winter afternoons in the Litchfield hills, the light turns white-gold just before it fades. I looked down into the valley at the eerie lake below. It was covered in ice, a perfect oval reflection of the dying sun. In seconds it was dark—it goes like that, the light in winter, in a whisper. I drove on. I had just left a gathering, filled with couples, all happy, it seemed, all loving. A powerful longing overcame me, and I put my hand out to touch, and kept it there on the empty plastic car seat at my side.

I would become ill a few weeks later. I drove back to the city and fell into bed, feverish and exhausted. The following Tuesday I walked over to my analyst's office and plunked myself down on the couch. In analysis you lie prone, staring at the ceiling, the psychoanalyst a somber presence somewhere behind your head. It is an amazing process, one in which ultimately I learned to speak from my inner being. There was no face to look at, no expres-

227

sion to see and try to manipulate, no feedback to cause me to edit my thoughts and words. In analysis with Dr. Marshall I was left no option but to find expression for my most primitive self.

Today I told him lightly that I had been sick but now was better.

"Who took care of you?" he asked.

"Oh, nobody," I replied. "It's okay—I was fine."

"You must be sad to have no one to take care of you. . . ."

Sad . . .

The sadness washes over me and tears began to trickle down the sides of my face. I reach up with one hand to wipe them away, but suddenly I feel floaty, a buzzing void in my ears, my blood pressure dropping, my limbs and extremities prickly and loose. It is almost as if I had been hypnotized, but I have not. I am instead letting go of the conscious experience, moving into a pre-conscious, pre-verbal state of existence. I am entering a free-floating limbo, completely open, unguarded, and without defense. My hands move to cover my navel—I have to cover it, for I have the most intense feeling that it is bare and naked and exposed.

I am very frightened, but it is also familiar, this feeling, so old, so known . . . I remember it, remember being there before, remember it as an integral part of me.

"I feel . . ."

"You feel . . ."

"Naked, bare . . . it is all white, everything, where I am. I am surrounded in whiteness. But my navel, I have to protect it, I have to hold it, cover it . . . I can't . . ." I wanted to say, "I can't stay here, I am bare, without power, without protection."

"Stay there, stay where you are," says Dr. Marshall.

"But I can't . . . I can't."

What I can't do is speak anymore; I have no words—I have become suddenly pre-verbal, reverted to an earlier state before words exist, a place where there is only sensation. I stay there as he asks.

I don't know for how long, for time is immeasurable where I am, covering my midriff with both hands. Somehow I have been transported into this whiteness; it wraps me like fog. I am totally alone in an alone universe. For ever. But it is not an alien place. I know it well, knew it always.

Slowly I begin to surface, and my trancelike state to lift. I begin to hear the traffic noises out on the street and come back into my body, my body lying on a couch in a psychoanalyst's office on Third Avenue in New York City.

I don't need to cover myself anymore; I relax my hands and begin to feel whole as the blood flows back into my limbs and my buzzing ears begin to clear.

"I wish . . ." I say.

"You wish . . ."

"I wish there had been someone sometime to hold me, to rock me and hold me close. . . ."

From behind my head, Dr. Marshall says, "I wish I could do that for you, but you know that I can't, I cannot hold you."

Of course I know that. And I know finally, and understand, that no one can or will ever make up for the holding I haven't had. The fruitless quest is over, the nagging empty place acknowledged and accepted. I feel a sub-

tle relief. I try to sit up, but I am still faint and weak from the experience.

"Stay there, stay as long as you need to," says Dr. Marshall.

It didn't happen overnight. There was no surge of wholeness and of integration, no miracle. I simply came gradually to feel more at ease with myself, less needy, and infinitely more content with my solitude. For what my infant memory had unleashed was the knowledge and acceptance of my existential aloneness, the mystical aloneness of all human beings. There is no magical Other to cure or to complete—only the other that some people call God.

I had chosen to journey without that belief. And so I was on my own. It wasn't that I had given up the hope of a loving relationship but rather that I had given in, stopped fighting my fear of being alone. There are also rewards to being alone, which I was beginning to discover and which are difficult to describe. I am not speaking of the wonderful selfish aspects of being alone: eating Rice Krispies for supper, controlling the thermostat *and* the remote control, going to movies instead of films. I speak of something else, of a peacefulness, a quiet that leaves you open and receptive to the subtlety of beauty and allows you to take pleasure in it, to belong to it with a sense of harmony and of oneness. You can look at the same apple tree, in bloom or bare and gnarled in winter, the same sky, the same configuration of a beloved animal at rest, and they are never the same.

When I am alone, I am still. When I am alone, I take in; I simply am. When I am alone I am more *with* totality, more one, more connected. Eliot described it, this quietude and feeling of oneness, in "Burnt Norton": "At the still point of the turning world . . . there the dance is."

Another process originated from my birth memory. For I am certain that that was where I had gone, back to maternity, to a white hospital crib in an antiseptic white nursery, just born, my umbilical cord severed, my mother detached and disappeared. One day without ever having thought about doing it, I began to write, not the term papers or case histories or articles that I had written in the past, but a story. I wrote in the country, in a prefab house I had had built a few years after my divorce from Ray in what was once the Great Elm orchard. Only there in the peace and stillness.

I knew by now that for economy's sake I must make a choice between New York and Sharon—not much choice between a whole house and a one-bedroom apartment. I chose the house, and the quiet there that I had begun to relish. And in that quiet, the writing continued, a little story at first about my home in South Carolina and about a woman very like my mother and about the servants who worked for her. It poured out of me and there were times when I forgot to eat and fell into bed, spent, only to rise with the words already made in my head. All ready to be put down. It absorbed me. It thrilled me, this process of thinking and saying, of watching the characters spill onto paper. I had just turned fifty. I had yet to learn that writing is also hard work, aggravating at times, infuriating, frustrating, not fun, but consuming always.

"If you give your life to creativity, you give up forever the promise to be a good girl," says Erica Jong. "Creativity will inevitably lead you to give away dark family secrets. It will lead you into the labyrinth to face the minotaur." Maybe. At times I still feel that I am my dark family secret. What I have given up, though, are the walls—locked doors, trunks with lids shut fast. For writers must reach into those places and bring to light emotions and pain and trauma and turn them into a common unifying experience. And sometimes the hurt and shame that you uncover transcend the process, build strength, ennoble. Pain binds us more than joy, informs, corrects, cleanses, breaks down the musty barriers of complacency and self-congratulation.

Twenty-nine

I moved into my house at Great Elm with some trepidation. I had lived in New York for twenty-one years and made the closest friends there that I will ever have. I would miss Joan, Ellie and Bill, and Betsey (and Betsey's Lou) and Susan and Claudia, Rose . . . Ah, my friends! Still my friends despite all these moves and changes. And would I miss New York City? Not so much, not as much as I had anticipated, though I am proud that once I owned a tiny piece of Manhattan, that once I *belonged* there.

I had concerns as well about going home. Or seeming to go home. I hadn't actually lived in Sharon since childhood, and Great Elm was now a community belonging to other people. But still, it felt like retreat. My two sisters, Jane and Priscilla, lived in two condominiums in the big house. They were kind and accepting of me, so why at times did the move to Sharon feel so regressive? I needed time to reflect, to plan a future, to gather my strength in a safe and familiar environment, much as the toddler, running off to explore the world, stops, looks back, and retreats to the safety of her mother's arms. Without that sanctuary, the world is cold and lonely and threatening.

At first there were stretches of time spent simply look-ing out the windows—my house was filled with glass—watching the trees and clouds and the blue mountains behind. I planted a flower bed and then another. A friend gave me a bluebird house, and within days they settled in, flying from apple tree to apple tree, bright splotches of Walt Disney blue. Bluebirds look that artificial and magical.

I was still finishing my master's degree, having trans-ferred to the University of Connecticut. I began work as a therapist at the local mental health center, and there I met what coexisted with the pristine owners of the pristine colonial homes of Litchfield County. I met rural poverty and the dysfunction that stalks it. I heard stories of child-hood sexual abuse, of drug and alcohol abuse, of beatings and depression. There were times I felt the hopelessness of my clients, people who seemed to have few choices and little chance to change. There were times I felt helpless too in the face of their pain. I worked with one woman whose mother had tried to strangle her when she was five. And another whose father had habitually forced both his daugh-ters to perform oral sex on him: one to perform it, one to watch.

I manned a hot line for battered women, and before I knew it I was serving on boards again and fund-raising. I tried to help a young felon to become sober, and in doing so, forgot all the training I had received about maintaining boundaries. I met him first with an electronic cuff around his leg to alert the state police to his whereabouts. He had been an abused child, a product of foster care and of the streets.

I argued M.'s case in court before a judge; I routed him out of bars and faced down psychiatrists in attempts to

234

get him help. I panicked at his threats of suicide and, worse, at his threats against others. He was what some theorists call a primary alcoholic, a product of generations of familial alcoholism, with immediate onset, immediate blackouts, immediate loss of control. Sober, he was a sad, beguiling, anxious boy; drunk, he unleashed a deadly bravado and paranoia, and self-delusion and aggression.

I am in my flannel nightgown, reading in my bedroom, dogs dozing on the comforter at my feet. It is a cold, windy December night, black and starless. A bell rings and the dogs fly off the bed, barking, growling, and race down the hall to the kitchen door. I look at the clock; it is ten-thirty and I can see nothing outside. Hurriedly I put on a robe and walk to the kitchen door, the dogs scrabbling at my heels. I flip on the outside light. There is no one there. And in the driveway, no car.

I am frightened. I live on the hill by myself, no houses nearby, no one to hear me if I cry out. The bell rings again, short, impatient jabs. I tiptoe to the front door, knowing of course that I haven't bothered to lock it. "Carol, Carol . . ." I hear. And then there is pounding on the door and at last I recognize his voice crying "Carol? Carol?"

He stands shivering as I open the door just a crack, and I can tell immediately that he is stoned, a silly, sly smile on his face. At his side is a friend. The friend wears black leather and stares at me with opaque eyes.

"I can't take you in," I say, a part of me brokenhearted to see him lost and despairing—we have been through a lot together, M. and I. Another part of me remains vigilant; I am not afraid of M.—I can never be afraid of M.—but I am wary of his friend.

"I can drive you wherever you want. Let me get my

license." I don't want to say "purse," I don't want to interest the other one, the one who stares with the lifeless eyes.

M. sits with me in the front seat, the leather man in back. M. looks at me with his dopey smile. "I told him you'd help," he says.

He is thin, almost emaciated, his big eyes enlarged in their sunken sockets. His hands are dirty, the knuckles bruised—he has been in a fight again. He is wearing a thin gray windbreaker, not the down jacket I bought him last fall, not the gloves we bought together, not the hat and the scarf. And yet for now, the heater steaming up the car, he looks happy, content—the fulfilled look that only addicts have when their drug is close at hand, when their drug has been ingested. "Good, good!"—they feel good all over until it wanes and their synapses begin to cry, "More, more!" How can anything so fleeting as love win over the seduction of a drug?

I drive them both the twenty miles to Canaan, still in my bathrobe. M. turns before opening the door and reaches his hand to my face. "I'm sorry, so fucking sorry," he whispers, "so sorry, Carol."

I will never see him again, gentle, tormented boy, but I have heard that he is back in the penal system. Sometimes I think he feels safer there, safe at least from his own demons.

I continued to write: a tale about the symbiotic friendship of two women over a period of forty years. There are two spirited sisters in the story—parts of them remind me of Aloise and Maureen. That is the surprise in writing fiction—that you make up people who then become recognizable as pieces of your own existence. Well, hallo—I've met you before, I *know* you.

236

I met a man whom I could easily have loved, but he didn't love me; I met a man who loved me but whom I couldn't love, at least not in the way he wanted me to. They are still my friends. I bought Martha, a Maltese puppy to replace Calvin, in case Calvin ever decides to leave me. He is eleven. Calvin and my Westie, Daisy, resent Martha and hide under the sofa. I also adopted J-J, my daughter Carol's "cat from hell," who came with a strange medical condition that required immediate I.V. antibiotic treatment at the first signs of infection.

I had my friends from New York visit for weekends, Joan, Ellie and Bill, Betsey and Lou, Beth, my friend Shep. I gave small dinners, the kind I enjoy, in summer on the deck overlooking the meadow, in winter before the fire. I saw, and came to know for the first time, many of my grown nephews and nieces as they visited what we call Mimi's House, a condominium near the pool. Mimi is the name the grandchildren gave my mother. My brother Bill bought the apartment for them to give them access to Great Elm and to their memories of her.

Last winter I went to work at the Sharon Hospital. Hospital social work is like no other. This is what hospital social workers do: If a patient cannot pay the bill, the social worker is dispatched to the room to inquire about finances—never mind the terminal illness. If a patient has neglected to make out a living will ("advance directives"), one assures him or her of the wisdom of doing so, all the while reassuring them that they are not really dying this time—we need the advance directives for *next* time. If someone *is* dying and the family is upset, you comfort them and connect them to Hospice or to Grief Group. If someone is too ill or too frail to return home, you find a nursing home, the funds to pay for it, and then you "counsel" the patient of the great good sense of this move. Gently. If someone has a drug or alcohol problem, one helps him "agree" to treatment; if someone is delusional and out of control, you spend the afternoon restraining and reassuring her.

After an initial six weeks of high anxiety and clerical botches, I began to enjoy the work. The paperwork demanded of hospital employees is daunting, but I liked spending time with the patients, enjoyed working with the families. I respected the nurses. I liked the role of advocate and doing battle with the Department of Social Services (the State), and also with the doctors (God). You need a lot of moxie to survive hospital social work, and I found I'd had quite a bit of it all along.

One afternoon before I left, there was a commotion in a patient's room. A destitute old man was threatening to leave against medical advice. He was no longer able to care for himself, too sickly to survive alone, but he adamantly refused placement in a nursing home. A nurse asked if I might speak with him. His doctor had played rough. I'd heard him from the corridor: "You won't last two hours out there by yourself! If you want to live, you'll do as we recommend—we have a bed for you in the nursing home."

The patient, more agitated than ever, refused absolutely to be moved and announced that he was leaving "right now, just as soon as I get my clothes back on."

I knocked on his door and walked in. He leaned against the windowsill, head wrapped in his arms, his buttocks just visible as he sat against the bed, trousers half pulled up, T-shirt and shirt in a jumble on the bed beside him. He had disconnected his oxygen. It was evident that he was too weak to continue dressing himself and too proud to ask for help.

"Excuse me, Mr. ———, my name is Carol. I work here in the Social Work department. I understand that you're upset and want to leave. I wonder if you can tell me, tell me what's upsetting you so?"

He is a very old man, frail, ribs like ivory showing through his sallow skin. I have a special feeling for old men—a fleeting memory of him, the old man I once loved, helpless and at the mercy of others.

"I won't go. They can't make me. I won't go to that place." He does not look at me but keeps his head hidden in his hands. I suspect that there are tears there that he is hiding, tears that shame him much as he is shamed by what he has come to.

I sit on the bed just behind him. "No one can make you go anywhere. Where you go is your own decision. I'm concerned, though, about your health. You are not well enough right now to care for yourself."

There is no response except for the shaking of his head. I place my hand on his arm, very lightly. I do not want to make him more afraid, to add to his shame. What I want to do is put my arms around him, to hold and comfort him. But that is not professional.

"The home we have scheduled you for is pleasant and clean," I say, using neutral social-worker words. "We refer many of our patients there. We don't receive complaints. It's just over the border in Massachusetts. It's—"

"No! No! No-no-no-no-no-no—I won't go. They have rats, bodies on the floor, fifty people in a room, dirt . . ." He throws up his head, eyes wild, filled with fear.

"Willow Wood? Oh, no, Mr. ———; I have been there myself. It has gardens and clean rooms, and never more than two to a room—"

"Liar! Liar, liar!" He is screeching now. "I seen it on

239

TV—all the shit an' the garbage and people layin' on the floor!"

For a moment I am rattled by his anger, his wildness. I stay quiet to give myself time to think. Willow Wood— Willowbrook! Of course—it was there he thought he was being sent, to the scandalous, verminous home for the re- tarded, exposed so many years ago by the young Geraldo Rivera: lurid television shots of frightened patients wal- lowing in their own offal, of bruised faces and bodies and of filthy surroundings. No wonder . . .*

"Not Willowbrook—Willow Wood," I say. "I under- stand now, I understand. . . ." This time I allow myself to reach for his hand. He jerks it away, then gives it back, palm up, accepting. The fingers are cold through, and rough.

It took time and talking before it was straightened out, the confusion between the two names, the flight of years between then and today, between Staten Island, New York, and Great Barrington, Massachusetts. I am not certain that he fully believed me or, if he did, that he was able to retain the facts of our talk. I was careful to note the misunder- standing in his medical chart, careful to state that the pa- tient had not been understood. What he had not been was *listened to*—it didn't take a genius to discover the cause of his agitation. That is the most important part of what social workers do in hospitals: they listen.

I had made a full life for myself in Sharon, a life evolved in just four years of living there. The phone rang off the hook. It was becoming difficult to schedule the time to write. It was also becoming difficult to live within my means. (I have these financial "awakenings" every three or four years.) Was this why I had moved to the country, to

240

go broke and not have the time to think? The time to write?

What I *had* done was to stop trying to define myself. I had begun at last to *be* myself. I was not the many things I had thought I had to be to be valuable as a person or to be loved. In the absence of a lover, of an intimate relationship, I was free to evolve, becoming simply me. Who I am. I once heard a man say about becoming sober: "I was given permission to be ordinary." What a relief! Not to be better than or less than, to be special only as a part of. What is special is to be ordinary.

✿ *Thirty*

My daughters had married, both in one year, Carol and Jeff in May at the University of Virginia chapel in Charlottesville, surrounded by their college friends and by family. Carol wore the dress I had married her father in—my daughter-double, my Hummel baby, beautiful and loved. I wished for Carol and Jeff all that is happy and fulfilling—all of the happiness that seemed to have eluded me.

For once again I was faced with a startling sense of my own aloneness. There were Jeff's long and happily married parents; there was Tom with his wife, Sharon; Ray, without his new wife but with Serge at his side; and me, mother of the bride, divorced mother of the bride, very single mother of the bride.

Ah, well—I proceeded like a dimpled three-star general, giving discreet orders, directing the caterers, greeting guests and relatives, introducing former husbands, and pretending all the while that I didn't notice the nobody at my side, the no one to dance with, and the no one to share recollections of the day with.

That September, Anne and Peb married in Sharon.

242

Fifty years old and a lot to show for it: Buckley, Anne, Carol, and Tom (Great Elm, November 12, 1988).

The guests congregated at Great Elm under a green-and-white striped tent. How many tents have graced that lawn, how many parties, weddings, debuts? Jane was married there, and Maureen and Gerry. Maureen had her debut there as well, the house ablaze with lights and filled with friends. Reid, just graduated from Yale, brought along the Whiffenpoofs. One of Maureen's guests was Sylvia Plath, a fellow student at Smith College. In *Letters Home,* a collection of her correspondence to her mother, she writes:

> Up the stone steps, under the white colonial columns of the Buckley home. Girls in beautiful gowns clustered by the stair. Everywhere there were swishes of taffeta, satin, silk. . . . The patio was in the center of the house, two stories high with the elm treetops visible through the glassed-in roof . . . vines trailing from a balcony, foun-

243

tains playing, blue glazed tiles set in mosaic on the floor, pink walls and plants growing everywhere. French doors led through a tented marquee built out on the lawn. . . . Balloons, Japanese lanterns, tables covered with white linen—leaves covered ceiling and walls.

My daughter Anne is radiant, married today to the only man she has wanted and loved. The candles on the flowered cloths flicker in the coming dark, the band strikes up, and Anne is swept into the arms of her father. She looks up into his face, her hair framed by the same lace mantilla that I and all my sisters have worn as brides, her delicate features mirroring his. He bends his head to her, holding her close as if to make up for the years of separation—and, yes, Tom still looks exactly like Michelangelo's David.

Our son Tom finished law school and returned to Washington to work in the legal department of the Environmental Protection Agency. He is happy there, successful at work and dating a fine young woman. Buckley moved to Richmond to be nearer his father and to complete a graduate program in education. My sons are coming to know the father they missed for so many years. Our son Buckley is also friends with a fine young woman. And I? I feel, at last, that I am a friend to both my sons and a friend to my daughters.

Last winter my daughter Carol asked me to be with her in Tucson when she gave birth to her first child. I was touched that she wanted me there, but also anxious. I have had four children and yet never actually witnessed a birth.

Carol manages a restaurant, and she continued to work there throughout her pregnancy. She worked there throughout her early contractions. She worked throughout

244

her middling ones. She worked and worked, and so did the baby. The contractions came more regularly, they came a little harder. . . .

Her due date was February 6. Jeff and I shared some desultory Chinese take-out, waiting for Carol to call. We kept each other's spirits up; we kept each other calm. Carol didn't call; instead she arrived home, rather cool, just a touch condescending in response to my anxious questions. Jeff, of course, is cool as can be himself. Jeff is a physician. "Well, he asked jokingly, "how many contractions have you had since sitting down?"

"About five," said Carol. Five—she'd been home for fifteen minutes.

I bite my tongue, I sit on my hands, I finally remove myself and lie on the bed fully clothed, waiting. It begins a few minutes after midnight—the real thing. We race to the hospital and the twenty minutes it takes to get there feels like two hours. That's how long twenty minutes feels when your daughter is in pain. Every time I hear her gasp, I feel an ache and my stomach tightens and my breathing becomes shallow.

I share what is happening to my child. I remember having babies as if it were yesterday. I remember her own birth and my joy that she was well and whole. I am also in awe of her, my baby daughter, so strong, so stoic, and so deeply infused with love. Sometimes I stand at her head, touching her forehead; Jeff sits below, holding her hand. When the pains come, we trade places, for he is a far better coach than I, encouraging and monitoring her breathing. Sweat streaks her hair, her cheeks are flushed. She strains, leaving us both behind, becoming one with the momentum of her borning child. The infant emerges, head down, an

245

unidentifiable membrane, and then—flip!—she turns over and a tiny face appears, eyes and nose, tiny clenched hands, an open mouth crying in outrage and surprise.

Carol and Jeff are generous with me—they give me little Priscilla to hold when she is ten minutes old. They share her with me. I hold this little life in my hands, tiny shoulders and head cradled in my right palm. I think she is beautiful—she looks just like my own babies when they were born, all peach-soft and nose and fuzzy head. All hope, all beginning.

One of the few things that I have learned about life is that it is filled with wonderful surprises, as many wonderful as sad ones—that you lose and find, a door closes, a door opens. Nothing had prepared me for the strength of feeling my little granddaughter evoked. When Carol and Jeff visited last summer from Tucson, I slept with Priscilla in my bed. When they left, my sheets smelled of her—a soft, rosy smell, as soft as her delicate skin and being. I didn't want to change them.

I have also learned that children do mightily love their parents and that they forgive them a great deal. I will move to the North Shore of Massachusetts, to be a little closer to my daughter Anne who lives in Boston. She is gentle and giving, Anne, and her husband, Peb, understands that very well. He also has the generosity of spirit to share her with her unpredictable mother. For I am not, as my children often remind me, like *other* mothers. I say things that other mothers wouldn't; I make "remarks."

At last! For I have no one to please but myself.

Anne works by my side, nonstop, emptying carton after carton—my life transported from Connecticut in bubble-wrap and heavy brown paper. Maureen's daughter,

Priscilla O'Reilly, has driven up from Boston to help as well.

"Mom," says Anne, "do you really need five sugar and creamers?"

Priscilla, hearing the reproof in Anne's voice, cautions, "Now, Anne—careful, Annie!"

"Priscilla, do you need a sugar and creamer?" I ask weakly, ashamed to have brought so much when I thought I had left so much behind. I had surely given away half my life, sold furniture, silver, porcelain, jewelry, left behind an entire identity at thrift shops, in the homes of friends and family, at the town dump. Anne unwraps a framed photo of a beaming Buckley and a large dead fish; she unwraps a chipped plaster mouse that Carol made in kindergarten.

We begin to giggle, to splutter with laughter at all the silly things I have carted from home to home to home, objects treasured: a tiny silver tea set, a locket with a faded, sepia face, a perfume vial, a pair of Mexican dolls—as if memories actually needed objects to exist. And as if you needed memories to remember people. I see my husband Tom in the delicacy of Anne's face—see him often out-of-doors, fishing, working on the farm.

Ray lives in my mind, in the questions it asks and in the answers it will never find. My husband Ray taught me to question. His mother told me once that I had a Jewish heart. Is that why my closest women friends are Jewish?

And Maureen?

"Carol, Carol," she teases, "why so serious?" And then I hear her laughter and see the quizzical expression in her eyes, affection wrapping round me.

Priscilla leaves with her mother's mother-of-pearl First Communion missal—why have I had it all these years?—a porcelain platter, a floppy straw hat, wineglasses, a ginger jar—she flees before I can pile more things into her arms.

Anne and I have supper, decadent escargots served in my escargot plates and eaten with my escargot utensils, and, awash in garlic and parsley, take our aching, exhausted bodies to bed. New beds in a strange new house, not the minimalist retreat I had imagined—a house already cluttered with me. Tomorrow we will put Peb to work doing awesome tasks like setting up my computer and stereo and mastering the Black & Decker electric drill, an instrument that in my hands takes on a wild, destructive life all its own.

The boys will come up for a week and help me put my new house together. We work together, arguing only about the time it takes to get things done. Tom deliberates, I rush in. Buck races in, I slow down. They say they like it here, like the port town and the water and the salt marsh. I am relieved. I want to believe them, for though in reality it has been years since my children lived at home, I feel that I have uprooted them once again.

I remember that I made this decision to move from Sharon for myself. For what I think I have to do. I must disentangle myself, unmesh, to be finally, truly on my own, an anonymous person in an unknown place. I want to be no one, a person with no history, no definition. I want solitude and the freedom to write. You can want something very much and still weep to leave something else behind.

Thirty-one

I have just returned to my new house in Massachusetts from France, my first trip there in twelve years. A beautiful sojourn, surrounded by my brothers and sisters. We congregated there for the ordination of our nephew, Patricia and Brent's son, Michael Bozell. He lived for thirteen years at the Abbey in Solesmes as a Benedictine monk, and now he is a priest—the first religious in our family, the only religious of my parents' fifty grandchildren. We, the elders, Priscilla; Jim and his wife, Ann; Jane; my brother Bill; Patricia and Brent, who are Michael's parents; and the second generation, nine of Michael's siblings, nine red-headed Bozells and spouses; our nieces, Priscilla Ilel, Liz Riley, Patricia and Priscilla O'Reilly—all arrive in the tiny stone village of Solesmes in a cavalcade of rented cars. The bus that we thought would bring us from Paris, didn't. Some of us got lost and missed the lunch in Chartres; some of us got lost and missed Solesmes until long after dark. Our friends Kevin and Jo Lynch, driving from Munich, arrived at a totally different Solesmes, somewhere in the bleak industrial north.

Michael's good friends are here, from high school, a college roommate who flew in from Hawaii, and new friends, friends made since he took his vows at Solesmes, men who visit the abbey during the year and stay there a day or two or three with the monks, and take back into the world with them consolation.

My sister Patricia and her husband, Brent, arrived earlier to prepare the celebrations. On the first evening we congregated at a fifteenth-century manor house for a banquet in Michael's honor. Only Michael was not there, for he lives cloistered and apart from the world.

We were served wine or mineral water with hors d'oeuvres in a long room with a vibrant tapestry of ocher red and greens covering the walls, a fire blazing at one end, and there in two regal chairs Brent and I conversed. We were comfortable with each other as Brent and I always are. My family tonight was radiant, happy to be together, happy for Patricia, for Brent—for of all of us, they have kept the faith most devoutly, unquestioning and meticulous. They have suffered sadness in their lives, they have been plagued by illness, but tonight they are proud, Patricia, small and thin, with sculpted features and rose-soft coloring; Brent, stooped now, walking with a cane, humbled before the occasion of his son's ordination, a frail and good man. The nephews and nieces weave in and out, some I have not seen in years, kissing, greeting, hugging each other, some actually meeting each other for the very first time.

At the appointed hour—well, almost the hour, as some of our party was still finding its way to Solesmes—we moved into the dining hall; tables oblong and round set

with white linen filled the room. Patricia seated me between a psychiatrist (who else?) and the writer Ed Miles. It
was nice to be between two single men. It had been a while,
and I like the company and the admiration of men. In that
way I am like my mother. Alan, on my right, was charming—it was difficult to believe that he had toyed with the
idea of entering the monastery himself. He was worldly,
experienced. He flirted—he spoke to me about his divorce
and about the Incarnation and Christ's love. Ed, to my left,
was a gentle, quiet man. He is half Moroccan, half Puerto
Rican. The Muslim side of his family repudiated the Catholic side. They do not speak. I was attracted to Ed; I sensed
that he was an un-belonger, too. And on this occasion, my
faithlessness oppressed me. I could join only from a distance, as an outsider.

*The toasts begin. Brent toasting his absent son, asking us
to pray that night for Michael and for his vocation. My
brothers, Jim and Bill, also stand to speak; it is difficult
because they weep. There is sadness here, and I do not
think it is about Michael. It is about people gone and
memories past. It is about things unspoken and losses un-
mourned, about a family growing old, about lives that
never live up to the promise of childhood.*

*Priscilla moves us into laughter, toasting Brent and
remembering the old NR (National Review) days and
Brent's procrastinating ways. Brent was one of the found-
ing editors of the magazine, and Priscilla was his managing
editor. Bill and Brent, Yale debating partners, were the first
American team to defeat the Oxford University team; at
one time they were more brothers than brothers-in-law,
but that was then, before the distance set in. Life does that,
brings with it unpredictable shifts and changes.*

Gentle Patricia, with a grace that is uniquely hers, toasts those who are absent. She lifts her glass to my parents, to Aloise, to John, and to Maureen. I wish my brother Reid were here too—then we would be complete.

Reid telephoned me just before I left. He apologized for missing my birthday, October 26. "You haven't missed my birthday, Reid," I said. "You're thinking of Allie."

"Oh," he murmured, "how spooky!"

On our first night in Paris, Bill asked Jane and Priscilla and me to join him at Laurent for dinner. Oh, it was grand! I hadn't dined at a restaurant like Laurent since Ray and I divorced. I had a flashback, back to my days with Ray, a pang, a missing love.

I told Bill and my sisters about Reid's remark.

"Oh, yes, yes," said Bill, "of course, yours [your birthday] is April twenty-fourth."

"No," I answered, "April twenty-fourth is Maureen's birthday."

Spooky.

Back here, in my new home, I anticipate another birthday. I will be fifty-five on November the 12. I will celebrate at Anne and Peb's new home. I have been here for almost six weeks. On Sunday afternoon, my young neighbors, Alex, nine, and her brothers, Dakota, six, and Harlan, almost five, came to visit. Their mother, Lola, made me a welcome wreath and baked dog biscuits for the crew: homemade dog biscuits! Harlan, not one to be outdone, has also brought me two pictures from his coloring book. One is of a "snub-nosed tractor." A yellow and pink one. I have tacked it onto a beam in the living room.

Harlan thinks I'm a funny lady. He hasn't learned yet

that ladies in their fifties are allowed to be funny (and even to wear purple) and that fifty is okay. And very, very free.

Alex, short for Alexandra, is planning on being a teacher; she had also decided to become an artist but now that she has met me, she thinks she might become a writer instead. Alex is gentle and sensitive and accepts whatever you have to offer. I so hope she will learn not to. 'Kota likes most things, but not things with nuts. Ever! Harlan says he only likes grape juice, the purple kind. I also know Jack, the mailman; Richard who replaced the dead dryer; and Ralph, my Poland Spring delivery man (the faucets in my new house run hot and cold salt water). Today Linda will come to re-enamel one of the tubs that have been corroded by the salt water. Peter Welch, the plumber—he is coming tomorrow to replace some pipes, also corroded.

I have also met Dr. Grillo, the veterinarian—J-J, the cat, is on a course of tetracycline three times a day. It is a pink liquid, flavored with cherry—not J-J's favorite flavor. He has an upper respiratory infection; he has twelve lives.

In the mornings here in Newbury I let the dogs out of my bedroom, out the door with the sill that I have just discovered is rotted. They tumble out onto the fenced lawn, wiggling with joy and eager purpose. Don, the children's father, and Eric who lives down the road have built me a wonderful fence. No more leashes, no more marauding Daisy, the dogs can play and frolic as they want. I stand at the door and watch them, heartened to see Calvin move so easily, for my old pal has arthritis and is becoming deaf. He snores and snuffles at night and keeps Martha and Daisy and me awake.

The lawn rolls onto a marsh off the Parker River, a wetland filled with silent white birds. Tommy has sent me a telescope for my birthday so that I can identify them. So

253

Here in Newbury . . .

far they look pretty much the same, white and serene. It is the weather up here that is changeable, like Ireland. All day long the marsh changes color, from rose to gold to dun brown, to dark purple in the evening. Sometimes the tide washes in and instead of marsh, I am surprised to find a flat, shimmering lake at the edge of the lawn. Some mornings now the tall grasses are rimmed in frost, silver and stiff. Soon it will snow.

I distribute the dog food into three bowls, careful to recycle the cans, and watch to make sure that tiny Martha gets her share, though Martha is the most feisty of the three. But then, she is the smallest—she has learned to be tough. I make coffee and start the woodstove; I open the vents, lay newspaper, a handful of kindling, and two small logs. The fire flares, or doesn't, and as I sip my coffee I begin to think about what I am going to write today, what I have to say. Have I anything to say?

The house is quiet, only the hum of my computer breaking the silence. The dogs are sated and drowsy. Calvin lies at my feet on the tattered throw I lent my mother years ago, to keep her warm while she watched TV. J-J has escaped outside where Dr. Grillo says he shouldn't be. Calling him is futile—J-J is catching moles or crouched behind a tree, hunched, waiting for something of greater interest to come along. It is cold today, the kind of prickly cold that stings your hands and face.

Warm in the room I use as my office, I glance up and see that snow has covered the ground without my noticing. The dogs are still, content in sleep. "Oh, look," I want to say, "it's snowing!"